The NCTE High School [Literature Series]

▪ ▪

LIBRARY
SUNY GENESEO
COLLEGE AT GE

COLLEGE LIBRARIES

The NCTE High School Literature Series offers classroom teachers in-depth studies of individual writers. Grounded in theory, each volume focuses on a single author or work and features excerpts from the writer's works, biographical information, and samples of professional literary criticism. Rich in opportunities for classroom discussion and writing assignments that teachers can adapt to their own literature curriculum, each book also offers many examples of student writing.

Volumes in the Series

Zora Neale Hurston in the Classroom: "With a harp and a sword in my hands" (2009), Renée H. Shea and Deborah L. Wilchek

Sherman Alexie in the Classroom: "This is not a silent movie. Our voices will save our lives." (2008), Heather E. Bruce, Anna E. Baldwin, and Christabel Umphrey

Tim O'Brien in the Classroom: "This too is true: Stories can save us" (2007), Barry Gilmore and Alexander Kaplan

The Great Gatsby *in the Classroom: Searching for the American Dream* (2006), David Dowling

Judith Ortiz Cofer in the Classroom: A Woman in Front of the Sun (2006), Carol Jago

Langston Hughes in the Classroom: "Do Nothin' till You Hear from Me" (2006), Carmaletta M. Williams

Amy Tan in the Classroom: "The art of invisible strength" (2005), Renée H. Shea and Deborah L. Wilchek

Raymond Carver in the Classroom: "A Small, Good Thing" (2005), Susanne Rubenstein

Sandra Cisneros in the Classroom: "Do not forget to reach" (2002), Carol Jago

Alice Walker in the Classroom: "Living by the Word" (2000), Carol Jago

Nikki Giovanni in the Classroom: "The same ol danger but a brand new pleasure" (1999), Carol Jago

Editorial Board: Cathy A. Fleischer

Dana L. Fox

Shari Frost

Barry Gilmore

Sue Hum

Sonia Nieto

Derek Owens

R. Joseph Rodríguez

Susanne Rubenstein

Kurt Austin, Chair, ex officio

Kent Williamson, ex officio

To Kill a Mockingbird in the Classroom

Walking in Someone Else's Shoes

The NCTE High School Literature Series

Louel C. Gibbons
Brookwood High School, Brookwood, Alabama

NATIONAL COUNCIL OF TEACHERS OF ENGLISH
1111 W. KENYON ROAD, URBANA, ILLINOIS 61801-1096

Staff Editor: Carol Roehm-Stogsdill
Interior Design: Jenny Jensen Greenleaf
Cover Design: Jenny Jensen Greenleaf and Tom Jaczak
Cover Image: AP/World Wide Photos

NCTE Stock Number: 25519
ISSN 1525-5786

©2009 by the National Council of Teachers of English.

All rights reserved. No part of this publication may be reproduced or trans-
mitted in any form or by any means, electronic or mechanical, including
photocopy, or any information storage and retrieval system, without permission from the copyright holder. Printed in the United States of America.

It is the policy of NCTE in its journals and other publications to provide a forum for the open discussion of ideas concerning the content and the teaching
of English and the language arts. Publicity accorded to any particular point
of view does not imply endorsement by the Executive Committee, the Board
of Directors, or the membership at large, except in announcements of policy,
where such endorsement is clearly specified.

Every effort has been made to provide current URLs and email addresses, but
because of the rapidly changing nature of the Web, some sites and addresses
may no longer be accessible.

Library of Congress Cataloging-in-Publication Data

Gibbons, Louel C., 1968–
    To kill a mockingbird in the classroom / Louel C. Gibbons.
        p. cm. — (The NCTE high school literature series)

    Includes bibliographical references.
    ISBN 978-0-8141-2551-9 (pbk)
    1. Lee, Harper. To kill a mockingbird. 2. Lee, Harper—Study and teaching
(Secondary) I. Title.
    PS3562.E353T63344 2009
    813'.54—dc22

                                                                2009007887

Contents

■ ■

Permission Acknowledgments vii

Acknowledgments ix

Introduction xi

1. Where Life and Art Intersect 1

2. Examining Literary Elements 14

3. Engaging Student Readers 30

4. Examining Text Structure 53

5. Addressing Sensitive Issues 72

6. Responding to Criticism and Primary Documents . . . 79

7. *To Kill a Mockingbird*: The Film 99

Chronology 113

Works Cited 117

Author 121

Permission Acknowledgments

Boone, Buford. "What a Price for Peace." *Tuscaloosa News* 7 Feb. 1956. Republished with permission of *The Tuscaloosa News*.

Early, Gerald. "The Madness in the American Haunted House: The New Southern Gothic, and the Young Adult Novel of the 1960s: A Personal Reflection." *On Harper Lee: Essays and Reflections*. Ed. Alice Hall Petry. Knoxville: University of Tennessee Press, 2007. 93–103. Copyright 2006 by The University of Tennessee Press.

Lubet, Steven. "Reconstructing Atticus Finch." Reprinted from MICHIGAN LAW REVIEW, May 1999, Vol. 97, No. 6. Copyright 1999 by The Michigan Law Review Association. Reprinted with permission of Steven Lubet, Williams Memorial Professor of Law, Northwestern University.

Mallon, Thomas. "Big Bird." *The New Yorker* 29 May 2006: 79–82. Copyright 2006 by Thomas Mallon. Reprinted with permission of the author. Originally published in *The New Yorker*.

Acknowledgments

▨ ▨

I extend my most sincere gratitude to Zarina Hock and to Kurt Austin, for without their encouragement and guidance I would never have been able to solidify my ideas and classroom practices into manuscript form. Additionally, I am grateful for the input NCTE's field reviewers provided. Above all, I am indebted to my students—past, present, and future. They have given me a career more fulfilling and delightful than any I could ever have imagined. To them, I say thank you a million times over.

Introduction

Looking back, the idea for this manuscript grew from two separate events. The first occurred one afternoon more than a decade ago when one of my students voiced his objections to reading *To Kill a Mockingbird* because of the novel's racial epithets. The assistant principal to whom he spoke, an African American woman who had lived through the turbulence of the 1960s Civil Rights Movement in Alabama, tried to allay his concerns, telling him that the language is historically accurate and that the novel in no way condones racial prejudice. Instead, she tried to explain to him, the story focuses on the devastating and life-altering consequences that prejudice of any sort creates for both an individual and for the larger community. Ultimately, nothing the assistant principal or I could say made any difference, and the student chose to read an alternate assignment, although he decided to remain in the classroom when his classmates discussed the novel and watched segments of the movie.

I left school feeling physically ill that afternoon, sickened by the thought that a student with whom I had always enjoyed a pleasant, mutually respectful relationship probably now considered me a racist. The positive result of this incident was that it prompted me to reflect, reexamine, and reevaluate the curricular choices I make as well as how I handle situations in the classroom. As teachers, we all do this every day, but situations such as a challenge prompt us to revisit the process with an even more discerning eye. It is this type of intense reflection that prompts us to prune and refine our curriculum in ways that generate new growth, producing a higher quality learning environment.

The second event occurred more recently when a student's essay about how life in the South had changed since the time period depicted in *To Kill a Mockingbird* placed in a contest sponsored by the Alabama State Department of Education and the Honors College at the University of Alabama. I was honored when my student invited me to attend the awards ceremony as her guest, and both of us were thrilled when we read in the invitation that Harper Lee would be making a rare public appearance. When the day finally arrived, we made our way across campus to Smith Hall, where the luncheon and ceremony were held in a huge, airy room, brightened by sunlight streaming through floor-to-ceiling windows. The room hummed with clinking utensils and the murmur of polite conversation as the attendees enjoyed the *Mockingbird*-style luncheon fare of fried chicken, green beans, and macaroni and cheese, but when the noise level fell abruptly, and then was replaced by total silence, we all knew that Harper Lee had arrived. In awed respect, all of us watched her walk the short distance from the back of the room to the front where she assisted in handing out the awards. At age eighty, world-renowned author Harper Lee was in our midst, taking time out of her life to travel several hours and attend an awards ceremony for high school students.

In the years since the publication of *To Kill a Mockingbird*, Lee has been characterized as reclusive, one who avoids the press, refuses to be interviewed, and stays out of the eye of a public who reveres her even more today than they did when her novel was first published in 1960. Although I cannot presume to know the underlying reasons for Ms. Lee's behavior, I would guess that she simply is selective in the ways she uses her time, lending her name and presence only to those events and causes that she deems worthwhile. For me, her appearance at the 2007 awards luncheon reinforced what all of us teachers know on some level to be true: we belong to one of few professions that enjoys the privilege of working with youth who will be tomorrow's leaders, and the choices we make regarding what we do in our classrooms every single day have the potential to live far longer than we ourselves as human beings will live. Just as Harper Lee is selective with the way she spends her time, as teachers, we must continually reflect, reassess, and reevaluate to ensure that we are making the most of every class period we have with our students. Sorting through myriad choices regarding curriculum, expectations for students, and classroom environment can be an exhausting, time-consuming process, and one for which we seldom receive reinforcement or validation. We possess the power to impact our students' life experiences, both for the better and for the worse, and we bear the responsibility of wielding this power in the wisest, most productive manner possible.

And as for the student I mentioned earlier, he eventually participated in some of our discussion of *To Kill a Mockingbird*, though I do not know whether he ever read any of the novel. Later in the year, he left a note in my box inviting me to judge a piñata contest his Spanish class was hosting, signing it "Love, Jason."* I took his closing as a sign that at the very least he didn't hate me, and I have to hope he understood the reasons why I chose *To Kill a Mockingbird* as a text worthy of study as one of our class novels.

For a multitude of reasons, the novel remains relevant to today's society, to today's youth. Scout, a female Huck Finn of sorts,

---

*I have added pseudonyms in place of actual student names in most cases.

comes of age during a transitional phase in southern society as antiquated customs and ways of the Old South are pushed aside by the emerging New South. Like Scout, our students live in an American society characterized by flux and diversity, with twentieth-century customs and mindsets expanding and changing to fit the emerging demands of the twenty-first century. The fact that I am writing this introduction a month after the election of the first African American president of the United States is synchronous with the novel's timeless themes of tolerance and acceptance. Undoubtedly, in their lifetime our students will witness societal changes of a scope unprecedented in history, and as is the case with Scout, our students' experiences will shape the adults they will become.

The chapters that follow relate some of my experiences reading *To Kill a Mockingbird* with students. The activities and work samples come from teaching the novel with different groups of students, at different times. More than ten years ago, a student's challenge to including *To Kill a Mockingbird* in my curriculum prompted me to rethink my teaching of the text, and I continue with this process of reflection every day of my career. Every semester, I make adjustments to accommodate differing ability levels, time constraints, and the inevitable change of plans that is so much a part of life for all teachers.

1 Where Life and Art Intersect

■ ■

Following the prosperity and complacence of the 1950s, the decade of the 1960s heralded an American Civil Rights Movement that was an integral part of one of the most turbulent eras of America's domestic history, ushering in unprecedented changes to the existing culture and society that would resonate for years to come. In February 1960, a Greensboro, North Carolina, lunch counter sit-in protesting segregation served as a catalyst, prompting similar movements throughout the South. Several months later in November, racial turmoil intensified as thousands rioted in the streets of New Orleans, protesting school integration. Also in November 1960, John F. Kennedy defeated Richard Nixon, becoming the youngest president in the history of the United States and bringing with him the era of the New Frontier, a time of youthful optimism and hopefulness that defined the decade's opening years.

It was in July 1960 that J. B. Lippincott Company published Harper Lee's novel *To Kill a Mockingbird*. Just as Atticus Finch predicted when he told Jem and Scout, "Don't fool yourselves—it's all adding up and one of these days we're going to pay the bill for it. I hope it's not in you children's time" (223), the 1960s were a time when the racial inequality and unrest that had been simmering for so many years reached critical mass. Throughout the decade, passions continued to mount and tempers flared as violence and

1

turmoil erupted all over the United States, but especially in the South, where a status quo predicated on racial inequity and oppression confronted challenges from every direction. Clearly, the American society that emerged from the turbulence of the 1960s was in some ways more cohesive, multicultural, and tolerant than it had been at the beginning of the decade, but before the tapestry of this new society could come together, portions of the existing society's fabric first had to unravel.

Historically accurate, *To Kill a Mockingbird* depicts the American South in a transitional period, one that was a sort of Dark Ages for minorities, spanning the post–Civil War period to the early years of the Civil Rights Movement. But as is the case with all progress and evolution, the transformation to New South from Old South did not happen easily. It did not happen overnight. And it did not happen without tremendous human sacrifice and suffering. In this way, the novel chronicles an era of American history through the timeless and universal appeal of its story and characters. Although Harper Lee maintains that *To Kill a Mockingbird* is a work of fiction, it clearly reflects the world of her youth: the rural South during the era of the Great Depression.

Despite the progress and societal changes that have taken place, racial inequity and underlying tensions continue to fragment American society, with today's society burdened by remnants of an outdated social order. Ironically, public education is one institution in which these inequities remain the most glaring, with students of lower socioeconomic and minority status attending school in underfunded systems and oftentimes being underrepresented in college and university programs. For all of our students, regardless of their background, reading and studying *To Kill a Mockingbird* provides a forum for discussing the sensitive issues and concerns many of them continue to confront.

Harper Lee's Life and Works

Childhood Years

Nelle Harper Lee was born in Monroeville, Alabama, on April 28, 1926, to Amasa Coleman Lee and Frances Finch Lee. Although the world now knows her as "Harper," she grew up as "Nelle" (pronounced *nail*); the name friends and family still call her. Like the character Scout Finch, Nelle Harper Lee lived in a small, Depression-era southern town and was the youngest child in her family. Just as Scout prefers tomboyish attire to dresses, author Marianne Moates describes the young Lee as a "rough 'n' tough tomboy" who had "short, cropped hair, wore coveralls, went barefoot, and could talk mean like a boy" (28). In the novel, Scout is quick to fight her father's detractors, and the young Lee did not shy away from physical confrontation. In a 1999 article in the *Monroe Journal*, George Thomas Jones recounts a fight he witnessed one day at recess when the elementary classes at Monroeville Elementary School were on the playground. A fourth grader at the time, Lee was playing a game of dodgeball when an older bully snuck up behind her and pulled her hair two different times. When he tried for the third time, she was ready for him, and landed him on the ground with a well-aimed punch to his stomach. His pride wounded at being hurt by a girl, the bully enlisted his friends to teach Lee a lesson, but after she dealt similar blows to the other two, they abandoned their plan to get even and left her alone.

Like Scout, Harper Lee was a precocious child who developed her interest in reading and writing at an early age. Alongside her childhood friend Truman Capote, the young Lee would spend hours outdoors with an old Underwood typewriter her father had given her, pretending to be a writer. Lee and Capote passed many days in a tree house in the Lees' chinaberry tree as well, acting out scenes from books they had read, including *Tarzan*, *Tom Swift*, and

3

the *Rover Boys*. Along with a mutual love of reading and writing, the friendship Harper Lee and Truman Capote shared would last throughout their lives. Clearly, these childhood years created an indelible impression on both authors and provided inspiration that is visible in many of their works.

College Years

After graduating from high school, Harper Lee attended Huntingdon College in Montgomery, Alabama, from 1944 to 1945, and then transferred to the University of Alabama. She spent the years from 1945 until 1950 as a student at the university, where she wrote for several student publications and edited *Rammer-Jammer*, a campus humor magazine whose name comes from "Rammer Jammer Yellowhammer," the university fight song. In some of her writings from her university years, Lee parodies the racially charged issues that dominated southern politics of the era. In 1947 Lee enrolled full-time in the University of Alabama's School of Law, and she spent one term abroad as an exchange student at Oxford University in England. In 1950, six months before she would have received her law degree, Lee moved to New York City to pursue a writing career.

Adulthood

While in New York City, Lee worked as a reservations clerk for Eastern Air Lines and wrote several essays and short stories. When friends provided her with a gift of financial support (that Lee insisted on repaying), she was able to devote all of her time to writing. In 1950 Lee submitted a completed draft of *To Kill a Mockingbird* to editor Tay Hohoff at J. B. Lippincott, who suggested revisions. By 1959 Lee had completed her revisions, and in mid-December of that year she and her childhood friend Truman Capote were together again. This time, however, no childhood games were involved: they were bound for Kansas to research a murder of the Clutter family that Capote had read about in the *New York Times*, gathering information he would use to write *In Cold Blood*, a seminal work in the nonfiction novel genre published seven years later in January of 1966.

The Publication of To Kill a Mockingbird

Despite mixed reviews, *To Kill a Mockingbird* became an instant success, and within a year of its 1960 publication it had sold 500,000 copies and had been translated into ten languages. Numerous awards followed, including a Pulitzer Prize in 1961. After Lee declined an offer to adapt her novel into a screenplay, Horton Foote undertook the project. Lee served as a consultant during filming, and the 1962 release of the film version starring Gregory Peck was nominated for eight Academy Awards, ultimately winning in three categories.

The Years Following the Novel's Publication

Although *To Kill a Mockingbird* remains Harper Lee's only published novel, her article "Love—In Other Words," about the selfless and unconditional nature of real, genuine love—whether romantic or platonic—appeared in the April 1961 issue of *Vogue*. Later that same year, the December issue of *McCall's* included the semiautobiographical story "Christmas to Me," about a writer whose close friends give her a Christmas gift of financial support to demonstrate their faith in her writing ability. Then in August 1965, Lee's article "When Children Discover America," celebrating America's beauty as well as the optimistic and open-minded eyes through which children see the world, appeared in *McCall's*. Twenty years later, another published piece of her work appeared in *Clearings in the Thicket*, an anthology of stories and essays from the 1983 Alabama History and Heritage Festival in Eufaula, Alabama, where Harper Lee made a rare public appearance, presenting a paper on Albert Pickett's *History of Alabama*. More recently, the July 2006 issue of *O: The Oprah Winfrey Magazine* featured "A Letter from Harper Lee," in which the author frames her recollections of her lifelong love of reading in the bygone, simpler time of her youth.

Interviews with Lee from the early 1960s indicated that she was working on a second novel, but in a 2002 interview her older sister, Alice Lee, stated "the second book never got beyond the thinking stage" (Mills 4). In the 1980s, it was reported that Lee was working on a nonfiction novel, tentatively titled *The Reverend*, which was based on the case of a minister who killed relatives to collect insurance money, eventually meeting his own death at the hands of a relative seeking vengeance. To date, however, Lee has not published a second novel.

Following the success of both the print and film versions of *To Kill a Mockingbird*, a curious public and intrusive press have prompted Harper Lee to virtually withdraw from public life, and in the years that have followed *To Kill a Mockingbird's* initial publication she has granted few interviews. For many years Lee divided her time between her New York residence and a Monroeville, Alabama, home she shared with her sister, Alice. Since having a stroke in 2008, Lee has resided in an assisted-living facility in Monroeville. Undoubtedly, Lee has earned her right to privacy, or in the words of Rheta Grimsley Johnson, "How many Pulitzer-winning, perennial best sellers does a body have to write to satisfy the hordes, anyway?" (A/11).

Establishing a Context: My Teaching Environment
Alabama, Then and Now

> There are no clearly defined seasons in South Alabama; summer drifts into autumn, and autumn is sometimes never followed by winter, but turns to a days-old spring that melts into summer again. (Lee 59)

Although Brookwood, Alabama, located in the west-central part of the state, lies farther north than the fictional Maycomb, changing seasons have little effect on the scenery here. In fact, the scenery has not changed much during the years that I've driven the sixteen-mile stretch of Alabama Highway 216 that separates my home from Brookwood High School where I teach English. Entering the town limits, I pass houses and trailers; the community center and surrounding ball fields of the town park; the post office (closed from noon until one o'clock every day); the town hall, service stations; a feed store, hardware store, and a popular local restaurant that is "Home of the Panther Burger" (our school's mascot).

Although a snapshot would reveal a rural school, typical of so many across America, outward appearances can be deceiving. Technology connects our school with the world beyond our small community, and our geographical proximity to a major university and the state's largest city keeps us in step with the times. Our student body contains many of the same cliques that are in most high schools—academically motivated students as well as apathetic ones; kids with perfect attendance contrasted with those who stay out for long stretches of time; athletes, independents, and all-around good kids. However, with a 7 percent minority population, what our student body does not have is racial diversity, which creates unique instructional challenges.

Challenges We All Face

As teachers, we hear so much about the challenges of teaching racially and culturally diverse populations that sometimes the obvious gets overlooked: How do teachers foster an acceptance for diversity in student populations in which the dominant mindset is that of mainstream culture? And perhaps even more important, how do we help students develop attitudes of acceptance, tolerance, and understanding that they will take with them when they leave our classrooms and enter the world beyond high school? This is quite a challenge, yet reading *To Kill a Mockingbird* provides students with opportunities to witness situations filtered through the perspective of their own life events as well as to experience events vicariously, or, as Atticus Finch says, "You never really understand a person until you consider things from his point of view . . . until you climb into his skin and walk around in it" (30). And that is exactly what we strive to do as we foster attitudes of tolerance in a safe and cohesive classroom learning environment where all students feel respected and valued.

Once the young people we teach enter the world beyond high school, they probably will never again be a part of any group that is as immobile as that of the high school caste system, yet most of them will live the rest of their lives in the shadow of who they were or were not during their high school years. One of my students captured the essence of this challenge when she said, "Trying to find your place in high school is like trying to find your place in a finished brick wall—there isn't one." So although we are powerless to change the overall social environment of a school, we can create safe havens within our classrooms, environments where a diverse student body can interact, learn, and grow together in an atmosphere of mutual respect. In this way, disparate students can discover that maybe they do have a few things in common, in spite of the rigid laws of a high school social order that govern their lives from eight in the morning until three o'clock every day.

The first class meeting of every semester, I look out into the sea of new faces that each class change brings and think, "These students are too different; they'll never get along; the classroom won't gel into a community. It's not going to happen this time. What will I do?" But somehow, some way, it always happens: the distinctly different backgrounds, temperaments, and personalities manage to get along and interact, at least for ninety-six minutes each day. Other than deliberately creating an inviting classroom where respect, trust, and optimism are the rule, and one that students can count on, I have nothing to do with the magic that happens. And every semester without fail, the cycle begins anew.

The Stories of Life: Everyone Has Them

When Harper Lee first submitted her novel for publication, editors suggested revisions because the book sounded too much like a series of short stories strung together. However, unrelated stories are the threads that weave the tapestry of our lives and shape the people we become. For example, novelist Stephen King has compared stories to "relics, part of an undiscovered preexisting world" (163), and these "relics" of childhood are exactly what I want my students to discover as a way of encouraging them to forge personal connections with the novel.

Additionally, sharing personal experiences helps solidify the classroom community. For these reasons, we preface our reading with related discussion to stimulate students' thinking and engagement. Forming a receptive, positive attitude toward the novel helps students remain open to the reading experience, since so many times they assume an assigned class novel will be a boring one. We respond to a writing prompt such as the one that follows before I distribute the books:

> Describe a recent event or one from your early childhood years that stands out in your memory because of the lasting effect—whether positive or negative—it has had on your developing into the person you are today. In retrospect, why do you think this event was significant in your life?

This quick-write, as well as many other writing assignments we do in class, is exploratory writing: unpolished, first-draft writing in which getting ideas recorded is the primary goal. We take ten to fifteen minutes of writing time—longer if I can see that the ideas are flowing and hands are flying across the paper—then discuss our reflections. If some students finish while their classmates are still writing, they can revise and edit what they have written, but they know in advance that this writing will not be collected and graded; rather, they will keep it in their notebooks where it might serve as the beginning of a longer piece later on.

When all the students seem to be close to a stopping point, I announce that we need to take another minute or two to wrap up our writing and explain that before opening the whole-class discussion, the students will turn to someone nearby and share in pairs. This serves two purposes: first, the social interaction serves as an icebreaker, and second, I can count on the students to exert some positive peer pressure if a classmate is reluctant about sharing a good story.

Rather than calling on students, I open our discussion by asking for volunteers to read or to tell about what they wrote. As the discussion progresses, I invite less vocal students to share their responses, but I have found that even though some students are reluctant to share personal reflections, they tend to open up once their classmates begin talking about their experiences.

One morning, Laura's partner Mark is eager for her to tell her story. After some persuading, she agrees, citing embarrassment as the cause of her reluctance:

LAURA: When I was little, I didn't mind or listen to what other people told me, so one time when we were at the zoo, they told me not to get too close to the walrus because it was sick. I just ignored the warning and got as close as I could anyway.

At this point Mark's laughing signals to the rest of us that the climax is coming.

FROM THE BACK OF THE ROOM, BERTRAM CALLS OUT: What happened then?

LAURA: The walrus threw up on me, and I had to go around the rest of the day in those stinky clothes. But it did teach me to listen to what people tell me.

After Laura finishes, she reminds Mark that it's only fair for him to share what he wrote as well.

MARK: Moving around so much when I was younger had an effect on me. Going to four different middle schools in different parts of the country was a way for me to meet lots of different kinds of people and, at the same time, I had to learn to adapt to lots of different situations quickly.

We all agree that adaptation is a necessary life skill, and Darren volunteers to tell us about what he wrote.

DARREN: When I was little, my dad wasn't around and my mom was always working, so I spent a lot of time with my grandma. I was really shy and didn't play with the other kids much, but I was really close to her—was a grandma's boy, you know. Then she died . . .

The classroom falls silent. All of us avert our eyes and wait respectfully as the 6-foot-2-inch tall, 175-pound offensive lineman struggles to regain control of his emotions.

DARREN: . . . and because of that, I'm really guarded; I don't trust people so I won't get hurt.

STACY: I understand that, but you can't go through your life being guarded with everyone. I mean, you should know that you can trust the people you've been friends with for a long time.

VANESSA: A lot of times you don't even know you're being guarded. I can relate to what Darren is saying because I'm like that. I mean, that's just me.

JESSIE: I know how Darren feels because I had a similar experience with my aunt. I spent last summer with her and had a great time, and we agreed I'd come back and spend every summer with her from here on out. Then she went in for surgery that was supposed to be routine, but . . .

The class becomes silent again, but Jessie continues talking through her tears.

JESSIE: . . . she died, and she was only 37. And now I tend to be really clingy to the people I care about, you know, because I'm so afraid I'll lose them.

Lisa has just lost her 21-year-old cousin, so she empathizes with Jessie. And so the discussion runs until I refocus the students' attention on *To Kill a Mockingbird* as a novel of the bildungsroman genre, one in which we will see the main character mature as a result of the story's events, just as the stories the students shared illustrate pivotal times in their maturation and development. Harper Lee has described her novel as a "love story," and clearly love lies at the heart of so many of the childhood stories the students shared with their classmates.

Separate Lives, Shared Experiences

As teachers, we understand that the appeal of timeless, classic literature lies in its ability to tap into the universality of the human experience and convey feelings and situations to which readers of all ages and eras can relate. When our students share ways in which their personal experiences relate to a text, they provide us with concrete, explicit illustrations of this interconnectedness. Additionally, by sharing experiences through class discussions, we forge the kinds of interpersonal connections vital to creating a sense of classroom community and respect for diversity. Our discussions remind us that no matter how different our backgrounds, the shared similarities in our life experiences provide a common thread connecting us all.

2 Examining Literary Elements

■ ■

We, as teachers, face so many difficult choices when we read literature with our classes. Most important, we want students to experience texts on an aesthetic level, broadening their perspectives through the vicarious experiences inherent in reading a well-written work of literature and developing a lifelong love of reading that will ensure their cognitive and intellectual growth. However, in an English language arts classroom, texts provide the vehicle for teaching multiple strands of our local, state, and national standards related not only to reading but also to writing, speaking, listening, and viewing as well. So how can we strike a balance that allows us to engage our students as active learners without alienating them as readers? For me, one of the more challenging decisions always concerns literary elements: I struggle with maintaining the delicate balance between "teaching" the novel and letting the students read and enjoy the novel, hoping that they will notice literary elements as they read independently.

Harper Lee's prose offers so many opportunities for teaching a multitude of literary elements: characterization, setting, symbolism, and theme. Although many students already possess a working knowledge of literary terminology, a brief review ensures that we share a common vocabulary. In most of the assignments related to the novel, I ask students to focus on the two elements that work together to form the novel's foundation and are essential to the novel's success as text as a whole: setting and characterization.

Setting

Although Lee maintains that the novel is not autobiographical, the setting—Maycomb, Alabama, in the 1930s—exhibits qualities that a visitor to Lee's hometown of Monroeville, Alabama, would have observed during this era. As was the case in many parts of the Depression-era United States, women and minorities in the rural South occupied a social position subordinate to that held by white males. While white women were viewed as the weaker gender, in need of protection from some of the unpleasant realities of everyday life, African American women and men occupied the lowest level of society, with most of them working in service positions that virtually guaranteed the perpetuation of their low status in the social and economic hierarchy. Additionally, scarce employment opportunities during the Great Depression created fierce competition among working-class southerners, to the extent that preserving the existing social order became a priority for many southern whites as well as a cause exploited by many ambitious politicians.

Historically accurate, Part I of *To Kill a Mockingbird* presents the milieu of the rural South in the 1930s: past-oriented, tradition-rooted, and staunchly segregated. It is no coincidence that Part I closes with the death of Mrs. Dubose, a relic of the antebellum tradition. Events in Part II introduce elements of change: Atticus and the children facing down a lynch mob, Tom Robinson's jury deliberating for several hours rather than several minutes before reaching a verdict, and Mr. Underwood's editorial indicting community prejudice. Without a clearly drawn setting, however, the novel's plot and characters would not seem believable, for the novel's overtly pervasive racism is a relic of an era that predates our students' life experiences.

To focus students' attention on the role that setting plays in literary works, we begin by reviewing the following definition:

> **Setting:** The time period and physical place that provides the backdrop of a narrative.

Following this review, we talk briefly about how authors establish settings in other works we have read during the term, such as the 1920s as the backdrop for *The Great Gatsby* and the contemporary setting of its companion young adult novel *Jake, Reinvented*. We follow our discussion with listening to a portion of an audio interview with author Tom Wolfe, a chronicler of contemporary American culture, in which he tells interviewer Laura Wilson that he "look[s] for a setting that is new and strikes me as kind of interesting, and then once I'm there, I wait for the characters to walk in." Students then respond to the following prompt, and their replies provide a starting point for our class discussion:

> **Prompt:**
> Brainstorm as many ideas as possible that you feel describe today's American society. After your list is complete, select one or more ideas you believe are particularly significant and discuss them in a well-developed paragraph. In your discussion, include how you see yourself in relation to the society you describe.

After the students have time to write down their thoughts, we begin our discussion. Not surprisingly, when I ask for volunteers to discuss what they wrote, we find that some of the students share similar ideas:

CAMILLE: Everything is very career-minded, money-oriented, and fast-paced in that people want to pursue a job that will lead to financial stability, but they want the success to come immediately.

REESE: Yeah, the ease that comes with technology has made people lazy and unwilling to take personal responsibility. I admit, I've been guilty of doing this.

TERRELL: I agree with Camille that people are more impatient than ever, and the desire to achieve and get things and information quickly seems to have caused lots of people to put aside their values and beliefs. I see myself as an outsider in a lot of ways because even though I want to achieve wealth and success, I'm not willing to sacrifice my morals to get these things.

Later, reading about the characters and events in *To Kill a Mockingbird* enables today's students to relive a bygone era in American history as they turn each page of the novel. When we finish the novel, students write in response to a prompt that extends our prereading brainstorming: how is today's society different from the time period depicted in the novel? Kayla's essay, excerpts of which are reprinted in the following, reveals her understanding of societal changes:

> "What is it, Jean Louise?"
> "Miss Caroline, he's a Cunningham." (20)
> What's in a name? In Harper Lee's fictional town of Maycomb County, people are known for their names, so the simple answer " . . . he's a Cunningham" is enough to describe what Walter Cunningham is like. Family relations mean everything, whether they are Cunninghams who ". . . never took anything they can't pay back. . . " (20) or Haverfords who are, ". . . in Maycomb County, a name synonymous with jackass" (5). Family tradi-

tions—along with stigmas—are passed down to every offspring. Preconceived notions and thoughts fill people's minds as they talk about the different families. This important fact creates a dynamic contrast to today's society.

Unlike in today's world, family names are everything in Maycomb County: Everyone knows the history of every family, and people are judged solely on their relatives. They have all lived together for so long that the mannerisms and quirks of each family are clear, as well as any oddities or characteristics: "the dicta No Crawford Minds His Own Business, Every Third Merriweather is Morbid, The Truth is Not in the Delafields, All the Bufords Walk Like That, were simply guides to daily living" (131). Family names pass from father to son, and along with those names come traditions, stories, and even shame. An example of this would be the Ewells, who have carried their tainted reputation for generations. However, in today's society, instead of being known for their families, people have to make names for themselves. Many examples of "making a name" can be seen in the work environment. People establish who they are as individuals to attain higher positions, which then affect how they are judged by today's standards. Individuality is celebrated along with diversity, and people have to establish who they are as separate and independent beings.

Independence is a goal many people in today's environment strive for, in contrast to Maycomb's population, which is grouped together unwillingly. One factor that contributes to Maycomb's stereotypical thinking is the way families used to live—together or nearby. For instance, at Finch's Landing, "It was customary for the men in the family to remain on Simon's homestead, Finch's Landing . . . " (41). In contrast, modern families are completely spread out. Many people move away from where they grew up, thus emphasizing the "making a name for themselves" idea. It is a way for families to start new or to start over. Also, many families are spread out, making it hard to tell what they are "known for." The negative connotations that a family name used to carry are not there any longer.

In Maycomb, prejudice comes in many forms, the most obvious being racial, but just as widespread is the prejudice against someone's upbringing and background, which clouds the minds of the citizens. One example of this is when Jem Finch wants to know about Walter: "He examined Walter with an air of speculation. 'Your daddy Mr. Walter Cunningham from Old Sarum?' he asked. . . ." (23). Jem only knows Walter from his father, not from the way Walter acts. Compared to in the town of Maycomb, open-mindedness is more prevalent in today's time where employers, workers, teachers, and peers do not worry about and are not concerned with a person's family history. Today judgment is based on attributes such as talent, work ethic, business status, and wealth—traits that did not play a key role in the minds of Maycomb's citizens.

To Kill a Mockingbird reveals the ugly truth of prejudice in its various forms. Since then, society has learned more about different cultures, resulting in a shift in the way people think about others. To Kill a Mockingbird influenced the way society viewed other human beings and made it clear that what can be difficult to see or understand in people's lives is viewed differently when described in the black-and-white matter of a book. Harper Lee took the social injustice of the era and presented it to the world in To Kill a Mockingbird, which changed perceptions and enforced the truth that everyone is created equal.

—Kayla

In this way, students draw inferences that help them relate the setting and mindset of the citizens of 1930s Maycomb, Alabama, to the world they inhabit today. Alice Lee, the author's sister, told one interviewer that Harper Lee "believed she had written something universal" (Mills 4). Clearly, even though more than seventy years separate our society from Lee's fictional Depression-era Maycomb, students are still making connections and seeing their experiences reflected in the novel's pages.

Characterization

Similarly, the characters in the novel are a product of the setting and emerge as realistic because of the time period in which they live. Though we discuss characterization throughout our reading, the more in-depth analysis comes after the students have finished the novel and have had time to digest each character's motivations and unique traits. Every term, we review the following literary terminology:

Characterization: The process through which an author creates imaginary characters so that they seem real in the mind of the reader.

Direct characterization: The author makes direct statements that tell the reader what a character is like.

Indirect characterization: The author reveals information about a character gradually, using his or her thoughts, actions, speech, and interactions with other characters.

Flat character: A character constructed around one or two ideas or qualities; usually his or her persona can be summed up in a single sentence.

Foil: A character that, by contrast, enhances or calls attention to another character.

Stock character: A stereotypical flat character, easily recognizable by most readers.

Archetypal character: One that epitomizes a well-known and easily recognized character type, such as the hero, the outcast, or the scapegoat.

Round character: A complex, multidimensional character that seems like a real person and, like a real person, may display contradictory qualities.

Static character: One that changes little, if any, throughout the narrative.

Dynamic character: One that changes as a result of the events he or she witnesses or experiences.

As we read and discuss the novel, students become more adept at using this terminology. Toward the end of the book, students work cooperatively to analyze a character from the novel and share their findings with the class. Depending on the amount of time we have, I assign this as an in-class activity, or if time permits, students create multimedia presentations in the computer lab and share them with their classmates.

For example, students talk with their group members and describe a character in the following ways:

- List literary terms that describe the character and explain why the terms are relevant.

- Describe the character's actions, reactions, interactions with others; what his or her speech and appearance tell the reader; the obstacles the character confronts, and how successful he or she is in overcoming challenges.

- Share a passage of your choice from the novel that illustrates what your group feels is the character's most dominant or strongest quality.

- Compare and contrast this character with other characters in the novel.

When we have enough time for the students to put together multimedia presentations, the following rubric (Figure 2.1) provides guidelines to help them organize the information they will share with their classmates:

	Outstanding	Good	Satisfactory	Needs improvement	Not included or unacceptable
Presentation teaches or reviews literary terminology and techniques					
Presentation demonstrates how the literary device(s) or technique(s) are used throughout the novel					
Presentation uses examples from the novel as supporting evidence to prove how the literary term(s) or technique(s) contribute to the novel's overall development					

Figure 2.1. Presentation organizer.

Regardless of the type of characterization activity the students complete, the discussion their work generates allows them to explore their ideas about characterization in ways that extend into generalizations beyond the novel. For example, this discussion about Mayella Ewell culminated with one student evaluating Mayella's psychological state:

STACY: Even though Mayella is mentioned throughout the book, we only see her in person at the trial, so she's a static character, definitely a flat character.

MARK: Yeah, she's a liar and doesn't know anything about how to act, like when she's testifying and thinks Atticus is insulting her because he's being polite.

SHANE: What doesn't make sense to me is that no matter how many times Atticus gives her the chance to change her story and tell the truth, she keeps on lying and covering up for her father.

PATRICIA: But what else can you expect, because her lie is what keeps the story going? To make her point about prejudice, Lee needs for Tom Robinson to get killed.

GIBBONS: Excellent observation, Patricia. You're reading like a writer.

BETH: And there's no way that Mayella would tell on her dad after so many years of being abused. She probably has Stockholm Syndrome because here her dad is a drunk who doesn't take care of his family and a child molester, but she won't say anything bad against him when Atticus gives her every opportunity to tell on him in court.

MARK: To go along with what Beth was saying, Mayella seems to be an archetype, a typical white trash kind of person.

Because the process of characterization involves the author creating fictitious characters in ways that make them seem real in the mind of the reader, the students' discussion indicates that Harper Lee has done this successfully, for they have no trouble analyzing the behavior of fictional characters just as they would do with a living, breathing human being.

Symbolism

As the students begin applying literary terminology to the characters and discussing them as if they are real people, their insight and analysis provide a segue into symbolism, another important literary element. Boo Radley and Tom Robinson are the novel's two "mockingbird" characters, because both do nothing but help others and suffer persecution as a result of their differences: Tom because of his race and Boo because of his idiosyncrasies. Additionally, in *To Kill a Mockingbird: Threatening Boundaries,* Johnson notes that both Boo and Tom are in cages of sorts, with Boo choosing to confine himself to his home, whereas Tom's confinement is literal, his incarceration (37). Despite these similarities, several contrasts exist, most notably the characters' race. While Tom is described as a "black-velvet Negro" (192), Scout's description of Boo's "sickly white hands" (270) and his white face creates imagery that contrasts with Tom's blackness. However, the manner in which Tom's and Boo's respective cases are handled reveals the greatest inequity. As sheriff of Maycomb County, Heck Tate is the first to arrive on the scene of the alleged rape as well as at Bob Ewell's murder scene. Yet Tate handles the two incidents very differently.

As white citizens, the Ewells' voices will be heard, despite the fact that the accusations against Tom are fabricated. Tom commits no crime but, as a result of the well-intentioned help he provides to Mayella, is accused and found guilty of rape. Then he is shot as he attempts to scale the prison fence, his only hope for freedom since he has little chance of winning an appeal. Conversely, Boo kills Bob Ewell to save the children, a deed that is both warranted and noble, but one that under normal circumstances would have prompted an investigation and gone to trial. However, because of Boo's shyness, Sheriff Tate rules Bob Ewell's death accidental and in the interest of doing what he considers to be the right thing, removes one of the weapons from the crime scene, tampering with the evidence. In this way, the markedly different handling of these two cases provides further evidence of the double standard predicated on race that runs throughout the novel.

Although the mockingbird emerges as an obvious symbol, by the time we reach the latter part of the novel, students are able to recognize other symbols as well. After working in small groups, one group's observation that Atticus's character symbolizes the changes the modern age will bring to Maycomb provided a segue into the following discussion:

CHRIS: Even though Atticus is a really good shot, we find out that he only uses his skill when he has to, like when the mad dog comes into the neighborhood.

TABITHA: Yeah, and the mad dog symbolizes the insanity in the town when it comes to issues of race, but unlike what happens when he kills the dog, Atticus can't save Tom because the prejudice was just too ingrained in people at that time.

GIBBONS: Based on what Tabitha and Chris have said, can we see any other places where a gun or rifle seems to be a symbol?

AMELIA: Well, Jem's and Scout's air rifles could foreshadow the dangerous time still to come.

JEFF: And it's like Atticus doesn't really want his kids to have the air rifles—Uncle Jack is the one who actually gives the guns to them—because it seems like Atticus realizes that they must learn to be responsible and handle powerful things, but he doesn't quite know if they are ready.

GIBBONS: But the trial forces both Scout and Jem to mature quickly, doesn't it?

Toward the end of the class after all the groups have shared their ideas, we discuss the following symbols and compile this list on the board:

- The fire that destroys Miss Maudie's house in Chapter 8 represents a sweeping away of all that is old, outdated, and useless, and suggests that change is on the horizon for Maycomb. Additionally, the complete destruction of the house suggests the firestorm that the Tom Robinson trial will cause in the Maycomb community.

- Mrs. Dubose, her camellias, and the tale about her having a Confederate pistol hidden under her shawl stand for the antebellum South and its customs and mindsets. Everything about her and her house suggest decay and stagnation, so it's appropriate that she dies at the end of Chapter 11, right before the trial begins in Part II.

- Atticus's warning that "it's a sin to kill a mockingbird" (90), followed by Miss Maudie's explanation that "they don't do one thing but sing their hearts out for us" (90), introduces the mockingbird as a symbol of something or someone that is inherently good. Throughout the novel, Boo Radley and Tom Robinson develop as virtuous characters misunderstood by society, and Mr. Underwood's editorial comparing Tom Robinson's death to the "senseless slaughter of songbirds" (241) fully develops the mockingbird as a symbol of someone good and just who suffers at the hands of an intolerant society.

Theme

The novel's most prominent themes relate to the unifying mockingbird motif, focusing on the destructive effects of prejudice and the idea that it is a sin to harm someone or something that does nothing but good deeds. Prejudice is manifested in other ways as well, such as in Aunt Alexandra's criticism of anything that conflicts with her values and in the social stratification that divides Maycomb society.

Other prominent themes relate to Scout's education and maturation. Although most teachers would be thrilled to find that a student possessed Scout's advanced reading skills, Miss Caroline criticizes the fact that Atticus has been teaching Scout to read and says she'll "try to undo the damage" (17). For this reason, when Scout goes on to say that "the remainder of my schooldays were no more auspicious than the first" (32), we believe her.

Another theme that runs throughout the novel relates to the harmful effects of religious extremism and to hypocrisy veiled in religion. Early in the novel, when Scout questions Boo Radley's reclusiveness, Miss Maudie offers the explanation that "sometimes the Bible in the hand of one man is worse than a whiskey bottle in the hand of—[Atticus]" (45). In the same conversation, Miss Maudie tells Scout about some other foot-washing Baptists who told her that she—along with her flowers—was going to hell because she spent too much time outside gardening and not enough time inside reading the Bible.

Later in Chapter 24, religious hypocrisy surfaces again when Aunt Alexandra's Missionary Circle gathers for tea in the Finch home. Scout overhears Mrs. Merriweather saying that they ought to "forgive and forget" (231), referring to the Tom Robinson case and the black community, who are dissatisfied by the injustice of the guilty verdict. This conversation as well as others reveals that many of Maycomb's residents continue to cling to remnants of an outdated social system, oblivious to the inhumanity perpetuated by their antiquated beliefs.

Of all the literary elements, the abstract nature of theme makes it one of the more difficult concepts for students to grasp. Some students either confuse theme with the work's subject or topic, or they think it is synonymous with a moral or lesson. However, once students grasp that theme relates to the meaning of the work as a whole, the lesson about human nature, or the way the world works that they gain from reading a work of literature, they are usually able to offer numerous statements of theme. Themes, however, are easiest to grasp once they have been fully developed, usually at the end of a work of literature. For this reason, as our study of *To Kill a Mockingbird* draws to a close, I ask the students to write about a theme they see in the novel. The following samples reflect two students' perspectives:

> Through reading *To Kill a Mockingbird* we learn to recognize that everyone is different from everyone else in some way, and if we can just remain open-minded to the differences that separate us, often we can learn from them. Atticus introduces Scout to this idea early in the novel when he encourages her to put herself in the other person's shoes and try to see things from his point of view. Through interactions with Walter Cunningham, Dolphus Raymond, Boo Radley, and her knowledge of the Tom Robinson trial, Scout matures and gains insight. In the end, she realizes that if people judge others and exclude them from

their life before they get to know them, they will miss out on many wonderful and enriching relationships.

—*Cecily*

One theme emerges above all others in the novel. Whether written or unspoken, society's laws are not always fair and just for everyone. This is most evident in the behavior of people like Miss Gates, the teacher who explains "DEMOCRACY" (245) to the children but says that it's time someone "taught 'em a lesson" (247); and the women of the missionary circle, who do everything they can to help the Mrunas in Africa yet see nothing wrong with the way they treat the African Americans in their own community. Atticus and his children suffer as well because Atticus tries to provide Tom the best defense possible, something to which he is entitled, yet many people in the white community don't think Atticus should be putting much effort into it. This kind of behavior shows that many times the rules of society apply only to a privileged few.

—*Robert*

Conclusion

One day toward the end of the term, in the last few minutes of class before the bell rang, Stacy said, "You know, this class has been a place where we could open up and discuss things as teenagers." Kacee added, "Yeah, I've never had a class like this; it's been awesome." But the environment we have all enjoyed has not resulted from anything I have done as the teacher; rather, reading works like *To Kill a Mockingbird* have provided a lens into the human experience and a natural segue to prompt discussion, encouraging students to explore insights related to their lives and personal experiences, both of which, in so many ways, have just begun.

3 Engaging Student Readers

The social and historical context of *To Kill a Mockingbird* is far removed from the world of today's students. Young people who have lived their entire lives in a society pervaded by technology do not seem to have much in common with children living during the Great Depression. So as teachers, it is up to us to help students bridge the divide separating their reality from the fictional setting that exists in the novel. Through careful planning, coupled with an inviting classroom environment, we can help most of our students forge the kind of personal connections with *To Kill a Mockingbird* that will make reading the novel an enjoyable, enlightening experience.

Coming to Know While Coming of Age

Scout's relationship with Atticus coupled with her proximity to the Tom Robinson case enable her to observe firsthand the devastating consequences a member of a marginalized minority suffers at the hands of a dominant white culture. In this way, Scout's coming of age in a society riddled with contradictions and double standards unfolds on the pages of the novel as a bildungsroman. Because our students are experiencing a similar process of maturation, writing and discussion opportunities enable them to explore and articulate the feelings about life, people, and the ways that life works that they are trying on and trying out.

Capturing Students' Interest: Responding to Writing Prompts

Anticipating the resistance some students feel toward reading virtually any book, I know that capturing their interest in the novel's first chapters is essential if I am to have any hope of engaging their interest and keeping them reading until the last page. For this reason, writing prompts link students' present day experiences with the characters and events of the 1930s era depicted in *To Kill a Mockingbird*. (A complete list of prompts follows at the end of this chapter.) Additionally, their responses provide a springboard to some lively class discussions. For example, sharing opinions about how men and women differ never fails to encourage even the most apathetic students to participate in our discussion.

> **Prompt:**
> When Aunt Alexandra's Missionary Circle meets at the Finch house, Scout realizes that she prefers the company of men to that of women because men seem more straightforward in their actions. Do you agree or disagree with her assessment of men and women? Explain.

After the students have had time to compose their responses, Darren opens the discussion:

DARREN: Well, any guy who has ever had a girlfriend will agree with Scout, because women are not straightforward at all. They beat around the bush, expect us guys to guess what's wrong with them, and when we ask what's wrong because we can't figure it out, they say, "Nothing."

CARSON: Yeah, and my girlfriend and I can get in a fight and make up, and I think everything's okay, but then later on we'll get in another fight and she'll start throwing up stuff from the first fight at me—and it's stuff I've already forgotten—like it just happened. I mean, women just can't let things go and move on.

VANESSA: Did you ever stop and think that from an early age, women are taught to distrust men? Or think about if a girl sees her father cheat on her mother, how is that going to affect her development?

STACY: Yeah, and think about how all the TV programs and talk shows that have women telling their stories about bad experiences with men affect everyone's ideas about relationships. I mean, everyone sees that stuff at one time or another because it's all over the place.

Throughout this lively discussion, I participate only as a moderator—or referee, if opinions clash and tempers begin to flare—but regardless of whether students are commiserating or arguing about issues of incompatibility that plague male-female relationships, they are connecting their experiences to the text and remaining engaged, which is the goal of having them respond to the prompts. Other times, their connections and reflections take a more personal turn, as Melinda's response illustrates.

Prompt:
The night Scout walks Boo back to his house is the last time she ever sees him. Reflecting on a relationship that, in retrospect, seems one-sided, Scout says, "We never put back into the tree what we took out of it: we had given him nothing, and it made me sad" (278). Describe a person who has come in and out of your life and helped you greatly whom you have never had the opportunity to adequately thank.

Melinda chose to write about the ways her mother's death shaped the young woman she has become:

> My mother's death really made me into the person I am today. When she died I was ten years old, a vulnerable, needy child, but since I didn't have anyone else to rely on, her death taught me that I had to learn to take care of myself. As a result, I've become much more strong-willed and self-sufficient—the kind of person I think my mother would have wanted me to grow up to be. Also, losing her taught me to be more compassionate, humble, and to appreciate everything good about every day and every relationship because nothing lasts forever. Although I know my mother would not have left me at such a young age if she could possibly have lived any longer, the effect her leaving had on making me the person I am now has taught me survival skills that will help me overcome other obstacles life will put in my way.
>
> —*Melinda*

Although having students write about ways that their own experiences parallel situations in the text provides an effective way of engaging them in the reading transaction, it is important to maintain a balance between fostering involvement and assigning work that will become drudgery. For this reason, I require students to write only one response for each day's assigned reading rather than requiring a response for every chapter. Additionally, assigning prompts in this manner gives them a broader choice of writing topics.

Extending Student Response: Writing beyond the Prompts

As we read the novel and write responses to the prompts, most of the students' writing is rather brief, usually only about a paragraph or a page long, at most. Because they have more to say about some of the topics, our culminating writing assignment asks them to revisit their responses to the prompts and choose one to develop more fully into a longer work of the genre of their choice: a short story, essay, personal narrative, poem, or another format. This assignment provides students with a degree of choice, enabling them to display their unique strengths. I have included a rap composed by Andrew, a student who transferred mid-year to my school from Chicago. Besides the difficulties he experienced adjusting to a small-town, rural environment, Andrew's reading and writing skills were at a rudimentary, functional level. For example, he managed to complete the research paper assignment only after I wrote out the first few paragraphs for him, with Andrew saying aloud what he was trying to express as I wrote down his ideas in sentence form. However, he was one of the first students to finish the extension writing assignment since it allowed him to capitalize on his interest in music. The *To Kill a Mockingbird* rap he wrote appears below:

> Here is a little story that you know I heard,
> A real good book called *To Kill a Mockingbird*.
> The whole book is about struggle and then glory,
> I'm telling you from the heart that it's a real good story.
> Now you heard all these stories that said Boo Radley was bad,
> His dad kept him in house; now that was very sad.
> Out of all things you could find in a tree, I found gum, a watch,
>   and a carving of me.
> I think you should know that my name is Jem,
> You can see me in person in the black-and-white film.
> I'm a young man, all good and tough,
> Scout is my sister; go to her when it's time to get rough.
> I pulled this girl off of boys in school,
> If you mess with her, you've got to be a fool.
> She is a known tomboy around my town,

With her fists is how she gets down.
Now Tom is a black man whose one arm is short,
Been wrongly accused of rape and had to go to court.
He was defended by Atticus, in fact,
Who loves people of all colors, including black.
My father was put down and criticized for defending Tom,
Just a few people in town saw the changes coming on.
I don't know what's to come, but I'll be finding out,
Because there's a new generation coming up here in the South.

—*Andrew*

Like most teachers, I struggle to balance encouraging student choice and individual creativity with the practical need to rely on a uniform evaluation instrument, both as a way to prevent grading from taking over my life as well as to ensure equitable assessment. For this reason, I devised this rubric (Figure 3.1) for scoring the extension writing projects.

	Outstanding	Good	Satisfactory	Needs improvement	Unacceptable
Evidence of time and effort spent					
Individual creativity					
Evidence of revising					
Grammar, spelling, and mechanics					

Figure 3.1. Assessment of writing projects.

Providing students with opportunities for writing about events in their own lives that connect to the literature they read taps into the egocentricity that dominates their lives. In this way, writing provides a means of encouraging even the most apathetic students to forge personal connections with the novel.

Student Inquiry Projects: Connecting Art and Life

Another dilemma arises with the question of how much historical background information students need to get the most out of a literary work. As demands on instructional time continue to increase, the decision always comes down to choosing the most time-effective and efficient manner of conveying relevant information to students. One day luck could fail me, but thus far every time we read *To Kill a Mockingbird* one of the students always asks, "Is this a true story?"—a question that usually arises during a discussion related to the Tom Robinson case. And that question provides a natural segue into an inquiry-based project, though there are numerous other ways to pique students' interest, such as through the K-W-L technique or a similar activity. Clearly, the student's question is yet another testament to the novel's verisimilitude: more than forty years since its publication, today's students read *To Kill a Mockingbird* as if it is a true story. Although Harper Lee has maintained that the novel is a work of fiction, students become involved in discovering apparent parallels between the novel's plot and characters and real life events.

To get them started, I introduce a list of research topics related to the novel, then post sign-up sheets around the room, enabling the students to group themselves and research a topic based on their interests. Because many students do not have access to the materials they need to complete projects on their own outside of school, we spend a few days in the school library working with print and technological resources. Working together, the groups analyze and synthesize the information they will present to their classmates, using the medium of their choice. Then they present their research through multimedia presentations, skits, panel discussions, or another format, followed by a class question-and-answer session. However, this activity can be adapted to suit any teaching situation, regardless of whether reference sources and technology are scarce or abundant.

Possible topics include the following:
- The era of the Great Depression
- Franklin D. Roosevelt and the New Deal
- Racial inequity and the judicial system
- The Scottsboro Boys incident and trial
- Harper Lee and her family
- Truman Capote's writing career and his friendship with Harper Lee
- The Civil Rights Movement of the 1960s

Evaluating the Projects

Because the work involved in assembling a group project should be shared equally among group members, I ask the students to evaluate themselves as well as their group members (Figure 3.2) after they have turned in all of their work and presented their research findings. The results of the evaluation are included in their grade (Figure 3.3). Invariably, I find that students take this process seriously and respond honestly and fairly in rating themselves and their peers.

	10–9 Outstanding effort	8 Good effort	7–6 Satisfactory effort	5 or below Needs improvement or unacceptable effort
Initiative and willingness to accept other group members' ideas				
Dependability and follow-through				
Contribution to the group's effort as a whole				

Figure 3.2. Confidential self- and peer evaluation sheet.

Students benefit from these inquiry-based projects because the process engages them in researching historical information they will teach to their classmates. Thus, they learn much more than if I were to try to deliver the information through lecture or another teacher-directed manner. Additionally, knowing that they will have to present their findings to the class motivates them to do a good job because no pressure I can put on them will equal peer pressure, which sometimes can be a positive thing.

Making Poetry Accessible through Bio-Poems and Acrostics
Some students develop a natural aversion to poetry, viewing it as hard to understand and impossible to write, so using bio-poems and acrostics provides a way to dispel some of their misconceptions and shows them that they too can write poetry. Although bio-poems and acrostics are easy for students to understand and complete, both types of poems require a working knowledge of

	Outstanding	Good	Satisfactory	Needs improvement	Unacceptable
Evidence of time and effort spent					
Explicit connections between the novel and the historical information					
Role in the group's presentation					
Grammar, spelling, and mechanics (*if applicable, depending on mode of presentation*)					
Confidential self- and peer evaluation					

Figure 3.3. Scoring rubric.

characters and events from *To Kill a Mockingbird* and require students to stretch their vocabulary for just the right word to convey their ideas. A basic template for a bio-poem follows:

Line 1: _____ (Character's first name)

Line 2: _____, _____, _____, _____ (Four adjectives that describe the character)

Line 3: _____ (Father or son or neighbor or friend, etc.) of _____ _ (Other character's name)

Line 4: Lover of _____, _____, _____, _____ (List three things/people)

Line 5: Who feels _____, _____, _____ (List three adjectives)

Line 6: Who needs _____, _____, _____ (List three nouns)

Line 7: Who fears _____, _____, _____ (List three nouns)

Line 8: Who gives _____, _____, _____ (List three nouns)

Line 9: Who would like to see _____, _____, _____ (List three nouns)

Line 10: Resident of _____ (Place name)

Line 11: _____ (Character's last name)

Cassidy composed this bio-poem to express her impressions of Miss Maudie:

Miss Maudie
Wise, caring, accepting, understanding
Neighbor of the Finch family
Lover of gardening, baking, tranquility
Who feels passionate, sympathetic, optimistic
Who needs a new house, more land, friendship
Who fears suffering, intolerance, prejudice
Who gives advice, baked sweets, perspective
Who would like to see progress, growth, and wider acceptance
Resident of Maycomb
Atkinson

—*Cassidy*

With acrostics, students write one or more words vertically down the paper, and these provide the first letter of each line. Some students choose to use names of places or characters, while others explore words related to one of the novel's themes. Chelsea chose to build her acrostic around the word *tolerance*, juxtaposing words describing the Old South with words that describe the type of future she envisioned for Maycomb and its citizens:

> Tradition
> Open-mindedness
> Lethargy
> Enthusiasm
> Racism
> Acceptance
> Negroes
> Caucasians
> Empathy
> —*Chelsea*

Involving students in writing bio-poems and acrostics provides a way of making poetry accessible to all students because the writing requires them to synthesize their understanding of the novel and express it through a creative medium. An added instructional bonus results from the demands the activity places on students' vocabularies: Soon after beginning the poems, they are reaching for a dictionary or thesaurus to assist them in finding the perfect words for expressing their ideas.

From the Page to the Stage: Rewriting Scenes from the Novel as Skits

Including a wide variety of activities that capitalize on every student's individual strengths is one way to make the English language arts curriculum accessible and engaging for the diverse students whom we teach. For this reason, many students respond well to an interpretive performance activity similar to readers theater in which they work in groups to write a script based on a scene from *To Kill a Mockingbird* and perform it as a skit for their classmates.

This is an activity we do after we finish reading the book, so all students are thoroughly familiar with the characters and events. Because each group chooses an event from the novel to adapt into skit form, the first few minutes when all the groups are discussing their ideas seems a bit chaotic. But they soon settle on a topic, and I record each group's choice to avoid duplication. Then the groups' efforts focus and intensify, with the students revisiting the novel with an eye for dramatic interpretation. A transparency showing an excerpt of Horton Foote's screenplay (Figure 3.4) provides a model for formatting and stage directions:

TO KILL A MOCKINGBIRD

FADE IN

EXT. MAYCOMB, ALABAMA – DAYBREAK

We are looking down at the small Southern town of Maycomb, Alabama. It is just before dawn and in the half light, we can see cotton farms, pine woods, the hills surrounding Maycomb, and the Courthouse Square of Maycomb itself. The CAMERA STARTS TO SLOWLY MOVE down to the Square. As we begin to see the stores and the offices which comprise the town, a young woman's voice is heard OFF CAMERA:

> JEAN LOUISE (VOICE OVER)
> In 1932 this was the world I knew.
> It wasn't a very big world, but
> neither was I.
>   (a beat)
> I was six years old.

THE CAMERA STARTS TO SLOWLY MOVE DOWN the main residential street leading away from the Square.

> JEAN LOUISE (VOICE OVER)
> They tell me Maycomb was a tired old
> town then, that people moved slowly.
> There was no hurry for there was no-
> where to go, nothing to buy and no
> money to buy it with.

continued on next page

Figure 3.4. An excerpt from Horton Foote's screenplay of *To Kill a Mockingbird*.

Figure 3.4. Continued.

During this THE CAMERA HAS COME TO REST ON the Finch house and yard. The Finch house is a small frame house, built high off the ground and with a porch in the manner of Southern cottages of its day. The yard is a large one, filled with oaks, and it all has an air of mystery about it in the early morning light.

> JEAN LOUISE (VOICE OVER)
> What I remember was that I was to
> begin school in two weeks, for the
> first time. What I didn't know was
> that my whole world was soon to
> change.

WALTER CUNNINGHAM, a thin, raw-boned farmer in his late fifties, comes into view. He is carrying a crocker [sic] sack full of hickory nuts. He passes under the oak tree at the side of the house as a young girl, six, dressed in blue jeans, drops from one of its branches to the ground. She brushes herself off and goes toward Mr. Cunningham.

CONTINUED

In this way, students dramatize their chosen segment from the novel using the stage directions and dialogue that bring the characters and events to life. After taking portions of a few class periods to write and practice, students present their dramatic adaptations to their classmates. After all the groups have presented their skits, each member of the class votes for the "Oscar" winner in the categories of best actor, best actress, and best adapted screenplay —although many more categories could be added—and the winners receive a small Oscar statuette and bonus points. Some of the winners choose to make an acceptance speech, while others decline this option.

	Outstanding	Good	Satisfactory	Needs improvement	Unacceptable
Scene depicted remains true to the original text					
Role in the group's presentation					
Grammar, spelling, and mechanics (in written script)					
Confidential self- and peer evaluation					

Figure 3.5. Scoring rubric.

Through the skits, student performers bring the characters from *To Kill a Mockingbird* to life and engage their classmates in imagining further details of the novel's events. This activity invites active participation at all stages of preparation and performance because it requires students to use their reading, writing, thinking, listening, and speaking skills as they prepare and then present to an audience of their peers. Additionally, involving everyone in the process of nominating classmates for the Oscars (and accompanying bonus points) makes the evaluative process (Figure 3.5) more inclusive, with both students and teacher determining the criteria for outstanding work.

This activity is easily adaptable to any setting and circumstances, whether students perform their skit in an open area of the classroom, outside on a grassy spot when the weather is nice, or in an auditorium for a larger group. Additionally, technology, such as computers equipped with word-processing programs or video cameras, can enhance students' efforts and assist them in producing truly amazing results.

Additional Resources: Complete List of Writing Prompts
Chapter 1
Scout establishes the setting by recounting some of the Finch family history and by describing Maycomb and its residents. Describe a place you spent time when you were younger, or tell a story that has been passed down in your family.

Chapter 2
Scout's first day of school does not go well. Think back to one of your first days of school—when you began the first grade or another important year, such as when you entered middle school, high school, or moved to a new school—and describe what stands out in your memory about that day.

Chapter 3
Miss Caroline's instructions that Atticus is not to teach Scout to read anymore seem ridiculous, since most teachers would encourage a child to read as much as possible, both in and out of the classroom. Think about your years in school and discuss a policy, rule, or procedure you have encountered that seems illogical or contradictory.

Chapter 4
Jem, Dill, and Scout play the game "One Man's Family" in which they reenact and reinvent the Radley family history, but when

Atticus sees them playing it, he expresses his disapproval. Describe a pastime, game, or other activity you and your friends continued playing even after being told not to do it.

Chapter 5
When Jem and Dill begin excluding her, Scout begins spending more time with Miss Maudie. Have you ever enjoyed spending time with an older person or another special person?

Chapter 6
Although at first Scout does not want to go with Jem and Dill to peek in the Radleys' window, Jem's taunting prompts her to go after all. Tell about a time when you went along with something because you were concerned about what other people would think if you refused. Was it the right thing to do, or did you regret your actions later?

Chapter 7
As Jem and Scout continue to find things in the tree's knothole, they debate whether they should keep the items. When do you think it is permissible to keep something you find, and when is it dishonest to do this?

Chapter 8
When Miss Maudie's house burns to the ground, little can be salvaged. If your home were about to be destroyed in some type of disaster—a fire, flood, hurricane, or tornado, for example—assuming all your family members and pets escaped, what three items would you try to save and why would you save them?

Chapter 9

In the altercation with her cousin Francis, Scout gets more of the punishment than she deserves and Francis is not punished at all. Has anything like this ever happened to you? Were you allowed to tell your side of the story?

Chapter 10

Scout and Jem are impressed when they discover that their father is a skilled marksman. Recount an experience you had when you found out that a parent or other person in your life had a special talent or ability and describe your reaction.

Chapter 11

Although Scout and Jem are frightened and disgusted by their contact with Mrs. Dubose, they benefit from it because her determination to conquer her addiction to morphine exemplifies her strength of character. Describe an experience you have had or a task you had to carry out that you did not want to do, but its completion produced positive results.

Chapter 12

When Scout and Jem attend church with Calpurnia, they become aware of cultural differences in Maycomb's black and white communities. Describe an event in your life that has expanded your realm of experience and heightened your awareness of cultural diversity.

Chapter 13

Scout and Jem are disheartened by the prospect of Aunt Alexandra coming to stay for an extended visit. Although we can choose our friends, we cannot choose our relatives. Describe a situation when you had to deal with a relative who is not one of your favorite people.

Chapter 14
When Dill arrives unexpectedly, Jem tells Atticus so that Dill's family can be notified. By doing this, Jem breaks "the remaining code of [their] childhood" (141). Is telling a secret or breaking a promise ever the right thing to do? Explain your opinion.

Chapter 15
Scout's conversation with Mr. Cunningham reminds him that he is Walter's father and an individual—a fact inconsistent with the mentality of a mob—and he tells the men to disperse. Have you ever gone along with something for a while but then reconsidered your actions?

Chapter 16
Although Miss Stephanie comments on all the people going to the courthouse to watch Tom Robinson's trial, she is among the throng of spectators. Throughout the book, she is characterized as a mean-spirited gossip and busybody who is always meddling in something. What is the best way to deal with people who behave in this manner?

Chapter 17
As Mr. Ewell testifies, his behavior reinforces Lee's negative characterization of him and of the Ewell family. From previous chapters, we know that Maycomb grants the Ewells special privileges and makes exceptions to rules to accommodate their behavior. Do you agree or disagree with this method of dealing with people?

Chapter 18
Even after Atticus disproves Mayella's testimony, she refuses to change her story and tell the truth. Considering her background, is she to be deplored or pitied?

Chapter 19
Mr. Gilmer's disrespectful treatment of Tom upsets Dill, so he and Scout leave the courtroom. Have you ever witnessed a situation when you were horrified at one person's treatment of another yet powerless to do anything about it?

Chapter 20
In his closing argument, Atticus says that "there is one way in this country in which all men are created equal . . . a court," and he goes on to say that in the United States "our courts are the great levelers, and in the courts all men are created equal" (205). Do you agree or disagree with Atticus's closing remarks?

Chapter 21
Although the jurors in the Tom Robinson trial deliberate for several hours, they return a guilty verdict, despite overwhelming evidence to the contrary. If a case with similar circumstances were tried today, what do you think the verdict would be?

Chapter 22
Tom Robinson's conviction upsets Jem greatly, and he tells Atticus that it's just not right. Have you ever been in a situation when you were upset by something that happened to someone you knew, perhaps only a casual acquaintance, even though you were not personally affected by the situation?

Chapter 23

Atticus remains calm after Mr. Ewell spits in his face and threatens him, telling the children, "see if you can stand in Bob Ewell's shoes for a minute" (218). When someone does or says something inappropriate, when should you respond, and when is it best to simply ignore his or her actions?

Chapter 24

When Aunt Alexandra's missionary circle meets at the Finch home, Scout realizes that she prefers the company of men to that of women because men seem more straightforward in their actions. Do you agree or disagree with Scout's assessment of men and women?

Chapter 25

Although Atticus presents the best defense possible on behalf of Tom Robinson, Scout notes that "in the secret courts of men's hearts Atticus had no case. Tom was a dead man the moment Mayella Ewell opened her mouth and screamed" (241). Describe a time when you tried to get someone to change his or her mind or to see your perspective, but the person was so closed-minded that he or she refused to even consider what you were saying. How did you cope with the situation?

Chapter 26

As Scout begins third grade, she says "the Radley place had ceased to terrify me, but it was no less gloomy, no less chilly under its great oaks, and no less uninviting" (242). Her words reflect the way a person's point of view changes as he or she matures. Has your perspective ever undergone this sort of change? For example, did you feel one way about something when you were younger but find that your feelings changed as you grew older?

Chapter 27
Although Bob Ewell is suspected to be the prowler lurking around Judge Taylor's house, the mystery remains unsolved. Describe the circumstances surrounding an unsolved mystery you have heard about or a mystery in which you were involved.

Chapter 28
As Scout and Jem are walking through the darkness toward the high school auditorium, Cecil Jacobs jumps out and scares them. Have you ever been the victim of a prank or carried out one of your own?

Chapter 29
In Chapter 27, Aunt Alexandra's description of the apprehensive feeling she has foreshadows Bob Ewell's assault on the children. In the aftermath of Ewell's attack, she tells Atticus, "I had a feeling about this tonight. . . . [T]his is my fault" (267). Tell about a similar experience you have heard about when someone's premonition came true.

Chapter 30
Until he understands that Sheriff Tate is trying to protect Boo Radley's privacy, Atticus wants the case of Bob Ewell's murder to be tried in court because he thinks it would be wrong to cover up Jem's involvement. However, many parents would want to keep things quiet and spare their child the trauma of a trial. How do you feel about parents who try to keep their children out of

trouble? Should parents ever do this, or should individuals always have to face the consequences of their actions?

Chapter 31

The night Scout walks Boo back to his house is the last time she ever sees him. Reflecting on a relationship that in retrospect seems one-sided, she says "we never put back into the tree what we took out of it: we had given him nothing, and it made me sad" (278). Tell about a situation involving someone who came in and out of your life and helped you greatly, yet you never had the opportunity to adequately thank the person.

4 Examining Text Structure

Every English language arts class contains a diverse group of students, and whether the class is a basic level or a more advanced one, some students will be stronger writers than others. For this reason, reading and discussing literary works in class enables us to demystify the writing process for students, many of whom view writing as a dichotomous proposition: A person is either a skilled writer or not, period. Because this mindset does little to encourage developing writers, helping students view a text through the lens of close reading enables them to grasp the craft behind the work as a whole. Indeed, it is positively overwhelming to imagine that even the most renowned works of literature began as a writer's ideas transcribed into printed words on a page and, through the reader-text transaction, gain a life of their own as scenes and characters spring to life differently in the mind of every person who reads that text. Abstractions assume concrete form through the reading transaction, and the resulting verisimilitude creates a sort of virtual reality for readers. The writer's craft makes this transformation possible, and literature provides the proof we need to convince students that there is a practical, utilitarian purpose for learning about the effects a writer creates through word choice, punctuation, and literary devices.

On the first day of class, I ask the students to write me a letter, including any personal information they want to share as well as discussing their perceived strengths and weaknesses in English class. Year after year, I find that the ones who view themselves as weak students include statements such as "I've never been any good in English" or "I have trouble with pronouns." Similarly, even those who believe they are strong students focus on mechanical issues, such as "I've always been a good speller." In every class, a few students will mention that they enjoy reading or that they like writing poems or stories, but overall, their comments reveal that they have distilled the rich array of the English language arts curriculum into grammar and mechanics, which should function as components of a balanced program rather than existing in isolation.

For this reason, teachers face the challenge of breaking down walls that students use to mentally segment the English language arts curriculum, mutually reinforcing strands meant to be woven together to form a complete tapestry, but that remain loose, disconnected threads in their minds. We want them to achieve proficiency and fluency as writers, both in terms of their own intellectual development and for the practical necessity of communicating their ideas through clear, coherent prose. Yet even at the senior high level, so many students remain developmental writers. How have students benefited from countless hours of instruction in the rudiments of grammar and mechanics if they do not transfer what they have learned to their writing? Probably we all agree that without the transfer, knowledge of isolated skills and rules is of little value.

Fortunately, carefully crafted literature provides an effective tool for helping our students forge these connections and heighten their awareness of how to use the writing tools they have at their disposal. Harry Noden describes this process in *Image Grammar* when he presents the metaphor of the writer as an artist, "painting images of life with specific and identifiable brush strokes, images as realistic as Wyeth and as abstract as Picasso. In the act of creation, the writer, like the artist, relies on fundamental elements" (1).

For all of these reasons, *To Kill a Mockingbird*'s rich prose provides countless opportunities for examining the way in which the writer's craft results in the effects seen in the finished product of the text as well as reinforcing students' intrinsic knowledge about punctuation and the ways writers use this knowledge to achieve desired effects in writing. However, I must preface this chapter with a word of warning: in many cases, students expect exercises that reduce naturally complex language structures into artificially simplistic patterns for the purpose of teaching a particular concept. They are comfortable with these types of activities because they know what to expect as well as what is expected of them. So don't give up the first time you ask your students to examine the way a sentence is crafted or to consider the effect a particular choice of punctuation creates, and they look back at you with blank stares. Model the process and nudge them to venture outside of their comfort zones; eventually, they'll catch on. Mine always do.

Examining the Writer's Craft
Clear, Vivid, and Precise Language
As soon as I pass out *To Kill a Mockingbird*, we turn our attention to the novel's opening passage. This is one of many selections that I read aloud to the students, pausing periodically to prompt discussion with questions that challenge them to reflect on the story's context and setting.

> When he was nearly thirteen, my brother Jem got his arm badly broken at the elbow. When it healed, and Jem's fears of never being able to play football were assuaged, he was seldom self-conscious about his injury. His left arm was somewhat shorter

than his right; when he stood or walked, the back of his hand was at right angles to his body, his thumb parallel to his thigh. He couldn't have cared less, so long as he could pass and punt.

When enough years had gone by to enable us to look back on them, we sometimes discussed the events leading to his accident. I maintain that the Ewells started it all, but Jem, who was four years my senior, said it started long before that. He said it began the summer Dill came to us, when Dill first gave us the idea of making Boo Radley come out. (7)

This excerpt enables students to grasp Lee's unique narrative style quickly, recognizing that the story is one from childhood and told in retrospect by an adult narrator. My guiding the discussion of the opening chapter also allows me to direct the students' attention to descriptive passages vital in establishing the setting, especially important since the novel's sociohistorical context grounds aspects of characterization and propels the plot. We begin by examining the underlying craft in the following description of Maycomb:

Maycomb was an old town, but it was a tired old town when I first knew it. In rainy weather the streets turned to red slop; grass grew on the sidewalks, the courthouse sagged in the square. Somehow, it was hotter then: a black dog suffered on a summer's day; bony mules hitched to Hoover carts flicked flies in the sweltering shade of the live oaks in the square. Men's stiff collars wilted by nine in the morning. Ladies bathed before noon, after their three-o'clock naps, and by nightfall were like soft teacakes with frostings of sweat and sweet talcum.

People moved slowly then. They ambled across the square, shuffled in and out of the stores around it, took their time about everything. A day was twenty-four hours long but seemed longer. There was no hurry, for there was nowhere to go, nothing to buy and no money to buy it with, nothing to see outside the boundaries of Maycomb County. But it was a time of vague optimism for some of the people: Maycomb County had recently been told it had nothing to fear but fear itself. (9–10)

First, I ask the students to identify the action verbs in the passage. As soon as they begin naming them, we notice that active rather than passive constructions make up most of the first paragraph—a testament to the power of showing through concrete description that we preach to our students! Then I ask the students to identify specific words or passages that create strong sensory images in their mind.

STACY: The part about the "streets turn[ing] to red slop" stood out for me because the picture I get is of people being pulled down by their surroundings, kind of like quicksand.

GIBBONS: What else did you notice?

JEN: To me, the word *boundaries* indicates closed-mindedness or limitations.

TODD: Yeah, it almost seems like the people are scared to leave, like in the movie *The Village.* . . .

CECILY: Or maybe it's more like they have everything they need in the town of Maycomb.

KATE: But that's bad—I mean, you should realize there's other ways of living than the way people are doing things in your own little world.

Kate's comment prompts me to introduce the idea of provincialism, a way of living most of the students loudly oppose, comparing it to living in the small town where we go to school for one's entire life and never venturing out, a lifestyle many of them say they would not want for themselves.

In this way, close reading and discussion help bridge the near century separating the world of today's students from the world of Maycomb's characters. Through sharing their perceptions about the importance of expanding one's realm of understanding and experience, the students are well on their way to achieving an awareness of the role that change and open-mindedness will play in the novel.

Examining the Rhetorical Effects of Literary Devices
Word Choice and Repetition

Excerpts from the Tom Robinson trial provide opportunities for examining ways in which Lee's use of repetition, coupled with careful, deliberate word choice, creates specific rhetorical effects. After we have read and discussed the chapters focusing on the trial (Chapters 17 through 21), I reproduce select passages on a sheet of paper so students can concentrate on them and analyze the effects the repetition creates. For example, the following quotation occurs in Chapter 17 toward the beginning of Tom Robinson's trial when Atticus is questioning Mr. Ewell:

> "Mr. Ewell," Atticus began, "folks were doing a lot of running that night. Let's see, you say you ran to the house, you ran to the window, you ran inside, you ran to Mayella, you ran for Mr. Tate. Did you, during all this running, run for a doctor?" (175)

The students work independently to compose responses to the following questions, which will serve as the basis of our whole-class discussion:

1. Why do you think the words *ran* and *running* are repeated so many times in such a short passage? Describe the effect this repetition creates.
2. What effect does the repetition of short, subject-verb-object (you-ran-X) sentences create?

Though some teachers might choose to omit the independent work and delve immediately into the discussion, asking students to analyze the passages on their own before the discussion provides them with an opportunity to reflect, clarify their thinking, and note their thoughts before we begin talking, as well as gives them something to refer to if they draw a blank. A few minutes later when I ask for volunteers to open our discussion, Sam points out the hectic, rushed feeling the passage conveys; then other students begin offering their ideas:

TODD: With using *ran* and *running* so many times, there seems to be a lot of commotion going on.

JEN: Yeah, the word choice creates an image of panic and chaos. It shows Mr. Ewell was doing everything *except* getting help.

RACHEL: I think Atticus was illustrating that Mr. Ewell was in such a hurry because he was worried, but not worried enough to run to the doctor. It creates a sort of mocking effect and makes Mr. Ewell sound like a liar.

BRETT: Yeah, kind of like what Rachel said, I think the repetition of *run* helps to show he was perfectly capable of getting a doctor, and this creates an accusing effect.

JESSIE: I think the repetition stresses Mr. Ewell's busyness but not his concern for Mayella. Atticus is showing the jurors that if Mayella really had been hurt, Mr. Ewell would have thought to run for a doctor out of concern.

AMY: Or, maybe there was no reason to get a doctor because she wasn't hurt—at least not until her dad beat her up.

TIM: Yeah, and this repetition that stresses Mr. Ewell's not running for a doctor definitely makes a strong point in the Tom Robinson case.

GIBBONS: Everyone has offered some keen observations, so what effect do you think all these subject-verb-object sentences create?

MARK: Stringing all those short sentences together creates the drama of running back and forth and re-creates the fast-paced action of what happened.

EMILY: Yeah, and since it's almost impossible to run that much, Atticus is discrediting Mr. Ewell.

NICOLE: Also, this creates a vision of where Mr. Ewell supposedly was running. I mean, it's a repetitive list of unnecessary activity that helps the jury picture everything that was happening.

BRETT: Overall, I'd call the effect tiring—both for the jury and for Mr. Ewell—making someone aggravated or tired so they'll tell the truth.

JAMES: It's just like what real lawyers do in court. They try to make witnesses mess up when they're lying.

Later, I ask the students to re-read Atticus's closing argument to the jury, paying attention to the words he repeats and thinking about underlying reasons for the repetition.

> I say guilt, gentlemen, because it was guilt that motivated her. She has committed no crime, she has merely broken a rigid and time-honored code of our society, a code so severe that whoever breaks it is hounded from our midst as unfit to live with. She is the victim of cruel poverty and ignorance, but I cannot pity her: she is white. She knew full well the enormity of her offense, but because her desires were stronger than the code she was breaking, she persisted in breaking it. She persisted, and her subsequent reaction is something that all of us have known at one time or another. She did something that every child has

done—she tried to put the evidence of her offense away from her. But in this case she was no child hiding stolen contraband: she struck out at her victim—of necessity she must put him away from her—he must be removed from her presence, from this world. She must destroy the evidence of her offense.

What was the evidence of her offense? Tom Robinson, a human being. She must put Tom Robinson away from her. Tom Robinson was her daily reminder of what she did. What did she do? She tempted a Negro. (203)

After the students have had time to read the passage and note their responses, we discuss their ideas:

KATE: The emphasis seems to be on the "code" Mayella broke. It's like Atticus is repeating the evidence over and over so the jury won't forget it.

JESSIE: Yeah, he's drilling into the jurors' heads that the wrong has been done to Tom Robinson, not to Mayella.

AMY: Right, and even though Mayella didn't actually break a law, she went against a way of life. But her guilt causes her to commit an actual crime when she accuses an innocent man.

GIBBONS: So let's keep in mind what all of you have been saying and look back at the third sentence. Why do you think Lee chose to use a colon there instead of punctuating it in another way?

SCOTT: The colon adds emphasis to the word *her* by saying she's white. The effect would've been different if a period was put in because it would create a less powerful pair of sentences

CHUCK: Yeah, if the author had separated the sentences, it would say Atticus does not pity her, but he means that he just does not pity her for certain things.

ABBY: And if she had separated the information by creating two sentences, the drama of the words would be lost.

JACOB: Also, using a colon is different from writing two separate sentences because it puts more emphasis on what Atticus is saying and causes a slight pause, so it can really sink in with the people on the jury.

CHUCK: Using the colon there shows how even though Mayella might seem poor and ignorant, there is no excuse for how she's acting because she is white, and that automatically puts her at an advantage over Tom Robinson.

JESSIE: And because of that, it stresses the racism in the town. If the colon didn't serve to connect "She is white" to what Atticus had just said, his statement would sound stupid, like he was stating the obvious, because everyone can see that Mayella is white, but the racism is at the heart of everything that's happening.

Many times my efforts at teaching student writers about the importance of precision in word choice have been less than productive, with students' efforts at revision reflecting nothing more than an extended session with a thesaurus and little understanding of the subtle connotations that separate appropriate from inappropriate word choice. For this reason, reading selections of Lee's novel with an eye for dissecting the craft behind her prose helps make the intangible aspects of the craft of effective writing more concrete in students' minds, enabling them to transfer techniques to their own writing.

Practical and Stylistic Uses of Punctuation

Commas

Of all the punctuation marks, the comma is probably the one that is used and misused the most. For this reason, most students benefit from some related review. When we stop to consider the numerous tasks we assign to the comma, it's easy to understand why students often have trouble with it. In *Eats, Shoots & Leaves*, Lynn Truss creates a humorous analogy of the multitasking comma, comparing it to a

> scary grammatical sheepdog . . . tear[ing] about on the hillside of language, endlessly organising words into sensible groups and making them stay put: sorting and dividing; circling and herding; and of course darting off with a peremptory "woof" to round up any wayward subordinate clause that makes a futile bolt for semantic freedom. Commas, if you don't whistle at them to calm down, are unstoppably enthusiastic at this job. (79)

By pulling example sentences that contain commas from *To Kill a Mockingbird*, we can ask students to determine the role a single or multiple commas fulfill in the sentence, and by doing this, students can discern rules governing correct comma usage.

To help students apply their knowledge regarding the ways commas can function, I reproduce some sentences from the novel on a handout, and then have them work in groups to discuss the ways commas are used in the sentences as well as the effects they create. I include the page number in case they want to view the sentence in context, and after the groups finish discussing each sentence, they write a rule—either using their own language or traditional textbook phrasing—to explain the way the comma or commas are used.

Example: Then if he's not dead you've got one, haven't you? (8)

Though most students write "the comma sets off a tag question," one group explains it by writing "a comma comes right before a short question stuck onto the end of the sentence, almost like an afterthought," revealing that even though they might not be able to recite the rule verbatim, they understand the comma's function, which is what matters.

> **Example:** What Mr. Radley did might seem peculiar to us, but it did not seem peculiar to him. (49)

Some of the groups explain the comma's function by writing that it "separates the main clauses in a compound sentence," whereas others state that the comma "is used with a conjunction to join two separate sentences." Another group explains that the "comma and coordinating conjunction separate independent clauses." Clearly, all of the students understand the rule governing usage, even though they may use different terminology in their explanations.

Once the groups finish analyzing the sentences I have given them—usually no more than five or ten—they apply what they have learned by agreeing on any school-appropriate topic that interests them and then writing some original sentences that illustrate specific comma rules. Todd, Mark, and Brittney play in a band together, so their sentences reflect their shared interest in music. For example, the sentences they wrote to illustrate compound structure and the use of tag questions follow:

> The Norwegian band Gorgoroth enjoys success in Sweden, but they are banned in many other countries.

You've already bought your concert tickets, haven't you?

Across the room, Megan, Brandi, and Laura seize the opportunity to vent their frustration over a recent breakup:

All the guys I've ever dated are like pigs, and they roll around in muck all day.

Overall, guys are selfish, mindless, smelly idiots, don't you agree?

Regardless of what they choose to write about, the groups' sentences illustrate their understanding of various comma rules. As they work, I circulate throughout the classroom to answer questions and provide help. Because collaborative learning groups encourage social interaction, many students who seldom ask me for help will speak up more when they are working with their classmates. The groups write their original sentences on a transparency to share with the class, so the prospect of having to present to their peers motivates them to work diligently at crafting good sentences.

Of course, this type of activity can be modified to illustrate almost any punctuation or stylistic concept and works well with students of varying abilities. For example, students with only a rudimentary understanding of commas could work with a group of sentences in which the commas all function the same way, or students who possess a more sophisticated understanding could analyze an assortment of sentences containing commas used for different purposes. Because students will bring differing knowledge levels to the task, this kind of work is well suited for collaborative learning. With some guidance, both developing and advanced writers will be able to infer rules governing correct usage of various punctuation marks.

Choosing to Break the Rules

As teachers, we have all experienced situations when our students have brought us books they are reading to point out a "mistake," a sentence they have found in a text whose structure breaks conventional rules. As experienced readers and writers, we know that authors sometimes choose to break rules to create specific effects, and having our students analyze the effects created when this happens provides a way of showing them why authors sometimes choose to go against conventional usage. To illustrate this practice, I ask students to read the following sentence and describe the effect the commas create.

> I had long had my eye on that baton: it was at V. J. Elmore's, it was bedecked with sequins and tinsel, it cost seventeen cents. (100)

The students shared their observations during our discussion:

SARA: Harper Lee was trying to make it sound like a little kid was talking, so she wrote it the way a kid would explain it.

JOSEPH: Yeah, she [the narrator, Scout] sounds excited because the commas create only a small pause between the sentences, making the pace quicker than it would have been with another mark of punctuation, like a period.

MISTY: Even though it seems like a run-on, the author is really emphasizing the baton by describing every little detail about it in a way that sounds like a little girl talking about something she really wants.

Having students examine structures that break the rules fosters growth in their own writing, for they begin broadening the range of structures they use. From time to time, students will bring me a paper they are writing, point to a sentence, explain that a fragment, run-on, or some other type of structure is needed to create a particular effect, and say they "just wanted to make sure it was okay" before turning in the final draft for a grade. I smile and answer "of course," pleased to observe a writer developing and gaining awareness of the power of rhetorical choice.

Learning from Master Craftspeople: Passage Analysis and Imitation

Just as the master-apprentice method works well for artists and other craftspeople, it can be an effective tool as we help students grasp the implicit artistry of syntactical variety and style coupled with well-chosen diction. Because some students find the idea of analyzing and imitating well-written passages difficult to grasp, I introduce the concept by asking them to tell me about a skill they have learned from someone who already knew how to do it well. Their responses—which range from a tale of improving a failing math grade by being tutored by a classmate to an account of learning about plumbing from an uncle experienced in the trade—provide a segue into asking them to analyze and imitate sentences or whole passages from the text. We look at a selection from a text, and I model the analysis and imitation process for them. Then, as students read *To Kill a Mockingbird* independently, they mark passages they find interesting with sticky notes in their copy of the novel, and then revisit them later to analyze how grammar, mechanics, and literary devices work together to convey meaning as well as to imitate the writer's form. The number of passages I require varies between five and ten, depending on the ability level of a particular group, and once students have finished with their passage analysis and imitation assignment, they share their work in large- or small-group format. For example, Julia chose the following selection from Chapter 2, when Scout begins the first grade, as one of her passages to analyze and imitate.

> She discovered that I was literate and looked at me with more than faint distaste. Miss Caroline told me to tell my father not to teach me anymore, it would interfere with my reading. "Teach me?" I said in surprise. "He hasn't taught me anything, Miss Caroline. Atticus ain't got time to teach me anything," I added, when Miss Caroline smiled and shook her head. (17)

Julia's Analysis

The irony in this passage is that Miss Caroline tries to deter, rather than encourage, Scout's ability to read at a more advanced level than her peers. Also, it hints that Miss Caroline has not received adequate training to deal with all the challenges a teacher will face. The conversation helps develop the novel's 1930s setting by setting up a contrast between the way an unusual student such as Scout was treated then and the way she would be treated now. In today's world, her individual precociousness would be valued and encouraged, but years ago all students were expected to be the same. Similarly, the use of "ain't" reminds the reader of the rural Alabama setting. Grammatically, it seems like the second sentence should contain a semicolon rather than a comma, but the comma doesn't slow the sentence down as much and conveys the feeling of a child relating a story about something that happened with her teacher at school.

Julia's Imitation

My sister finally discovered that I was upset and looked at me with more than slight concern. She spoke to me softly and said I should not concern myself with her affairs, it would interfere with my own life. "Don't worry?" I asked incredulously. "I can't make myself not worry, Beth. I don't have the self-discipline to be that much in control," I added, when Beth frowned gently and lowered her eyes.

In this way, the act of closely analyzing and imitating masterfully crafted prose passages enables students to expand their repertoire of writing skills and experience. A text as rich as *To Kill a Mockingbird* provides opportunities for illustrating almost any literary technique or grammatical concept. Jim Burke refers to the need for helping students develop their "textual intelligence" (56), or their sense of how writers employ different grammatical structures to create different effects in their writing. Further, Burke notes that the more students understand the way language works, the more rhetorical tools they will have at their disposal throughout the writing process. Undoubtedly, because our students have had years of exposure to text, they already possess this grammatical awareness on an intrinsic level; so as teachers, our task involves raising their awareness to the level of explicit knowledge they will be able to use in their writing.

The Value of Rhetorical Analysis

Reading a text for enjoyment should always come first, so we must strike a delicate balance when we base grammar instruction on literary models. However, well-written works of literature provide the best models for illustrating grammar and rhetoric as an empowering tool for writers. When using texts as instructional models, we must deliberately and explicitly show the steps in the composing process, lest our students feel intimidated by masterful prose and conclude that they could never achieve such powerful effects through their own efforts. Instead, we must demonstrate that writing is hard work for *everyone*, and even the most accomplished, prolific authors revise to achieve the powerful, just-right arrangement of words and punctuation that we read in the pages of a published work. In these ways, we can help students forge connections between the rules of grammar and usage and their utilitarian value in conveying meaning. Pushing students to apply what they already know on an implicit level raises their awareness of what real writers do. They may not thank us for our efforts, but they will leave our classrooms better writers than they were when they entered at the beginning of the term.

Additional Resources

Burch, C. Beth. *A Writer's Grammar.* New York: Longman, 2003.

As the title suggests, this reader friendly and entertaining text presents grammatical concepts from a writer's perspective. Burch's examples and activities are well suited to almost any teaching context.

Ehrenworth, Mary, and Vicki Vinton. *The Power of Grammar: Unconventional Approaches to the Conventions of Language.* Portsmouth, NH: Heinemann, 2005.

Besides presenting innovative approaches for teaching grammar in ways that will help students develop as writers, Ehrenworth and Vinton include practical tools for planning lessons and integrating grammar into the curriculum.

Heard, Georgia. *The Revision Toolbox: Teaching Techniques That Work.* Portsmouth, NH: Heinemann, 2002.

Recognizing how difficult it is to get students to revise their work, writer and teacher Georgia Heard offers a variety of strategies and lessons that can be adapted for use across the grade levels.

Noden, Harry R. *Image Grammar: Using Grammatical Structures to Teach Writing.* Portsmouth, NH: Heinemann, 1999.

Basing his book on the idea that both writers and visual artists create works of art using their respective mediums, Noden offers numerous lesson ideas and teaching strategies to help students realize the power that knowledge of grammatical structures and punctuation brings to their writing.

Schuster, Edgar Howard. *Breaking the Rules: Liberating Writers through Innovative Grammar Instruction.* Portsmouth, NH: Heinemann, 2003.

Schuster offers innovative ideas for helping student writers master traditional grammar and usage as well as ideas for helping them stretch beyond the conventional in ways that will enhance their writing.

5 Addressing Sensitive Issues

■■■■■■■■■■■■■■■■■■■■■■■■■■■■■■■■

Censorship and the Potential for Curricular Challenges

Along with its position in the literary canon, *To Kill a Mockingbird* holds an equally secure place in the list of frequently challenged works, and some teachers have found themselves immersed in controversy over including the novel in their curriculum. Despite these challenges, *To Kill a Mockingbird* remains one of the works most frequently taught in the secondary English language arts curriculum. Clearly, differences in individuals' perspectives can explain mixed reactions to the novel, but what are the implications for us as teachers of literature?

My Experience with a Challenge

From experience, I learned the importance of being proactive regarding censorship issues. I never expected to encounter difficulties in teaching *To Kill a Mockingbird* since it appears on the sample reading list in my state's course of study, and I had taught it without incident for years. Always, I addressed the issue of racial epithets with my students before reading the novel, stressing that societal changes have relegated racial slurs to the realm of offensive and inappropriate language. Additionally, because my curriculum covers American literature from 1900 to the present, *To Kill a Mockingbird* provides an excellent segue into the American Civil Rights Movement. Nevertheless, a young man in one of my classes voiced objections to the novel because of its racially charged language.

Although my assistant principal and I talked with the student who had raised the challenge, trying to explain the novel's merit and stressing that the entire novel focuses on the devastating effects of prejudice and promotes tolerance, he remained steadfast in his opinion. Although he acknowledged all arguments in favor of the novel, he believed that the fact that I would assign a text that included racial epithets signaled to the student body that I condoned the use of this language.

Eventually, this potentially explosive situation cooled down, and the student read an alternate text, but this incident raised my awareness of the potential every work of literature has to incite controversy and provoke challenges that cannot always be resolved amicably. My experience taught me the importance of preparing for curricular challenges *before* they arise, and after this incident occurred I resolved to take all the available precautions to diffuse similar situations that could arise in the future.

The controversy I just described remained localized and never went outside of the school building, a minor conflict compared to ones that have arisen in other places. Challenges such as this one have the potential to escalate quickly, requiring teachers to defend their curriculum to a group of parents, a board of education, or even the media. Clearly, the manner in which challenges are handled sets precedents, so it is vital that we English language arts teachers understand the importance of our role in preserving all students' freedom of choice.

Avoiding Challenges

Taking steps to avoid challenges is a process that begins at the classroom and school level, with departments agreeing on a selection process for literary works included in the curriculum. Then later, if parents or students object to a particular text, they can be given the option of selecting a substitute book with similar themes and comparable literary merit.

Even when no one challenges a text, still we must be mindful of the ways we address sensitive issues with students. Although opinions differ among educators as to whether racial slurs should be read aloud in a classroom setting, I avoid the practice because any resulting benefits are obscured by the embarrassment and anger generated by hearing the offensive language spoken aloud. Instead, creating a classroom environment that encourages and supports open, honest dialogue enables students to explore their feelings about this type of language.

Language and Characterization

Because *To Kill a Mockingbird* is a historically accurate novel set in the segregated South of the 1930s with a plot propelled by allegations of an interracial rape, racial epithets appear throughout the novel. Yet this language can serve as a teaching tool, prompting discussion about characterization methods and code switching.

For example, asking students to note which characters use racial slurs will help them discover ways that writers use language as a tool in indirect characterization. The speech of Bob Ewell, an uneducated, poor white man, contrasts sharply with that of the erudite Atticus Finch, a truly noble attorney who seeks justice for all people. Early in the novel, Atticus scolds Scout when she asks if he "defends niggers" (75). Although Scout is only repeating the language of her schoolmate Cecil Jacobs, her father teaches her that such language is inappropriate.

Miss Stephanie Crawford, along with an assortment of other townspeople, uses racial slurs, language that illustrates the inextricable relationship characterization and setting share. Mrs. Dubose rouses Jem to a destructive fury with her repeated remarks about his Daddy "lawing for niggers" (101), but Mrs. Dubose is a relic of the dying antebellum Old South, and her death at the end of Part I is no coincidence, as Part II signals the beginning of Tom Robinson's trial and a shift toward more progressive southern mindsets.

Calpurnia and Her "Double Life"

Interestingly, when Scout and Jem attend First Purchase Church with Calpurnia, she halts Lula's confrontation by telling her, "Stop right there, nigger" (119). As my students and I talked about the events in Chapter 13, the discussion centered on Calpurnia's behavior toward Lula.

KACEE: It's significant when she calls Lula the N-word because it's the only time we've seen her talk like that. In a way, she's fighting prejudice with prejudice, maybe because she thinks it's the only kind of language Lula will understand.

After Kacee finishes, I ask the students to respond to the passage on pages 125–126 when Scout questions Calpurnia about talking one way in the white community and using different language when she interacts with African Americans. Calpurnia tells Scout:

> It's not necessary to tell all you know. It's not ladylike—in the second place, folks don't like to have somebody around knowin' more than they do. It aggravates 'em. You're not going to change any of them by talkin' right, they've got to want to learn themselves, and when they don't want to learn there's nothing you can do but keep your mouth shut or talk their language. (126)

Darren, the only African American student in the class, is the first to respond.

DARREN: I know I talk a lot different at work than I do at school and other places, 'cause of the stupid, ignorant people I work with.

SHANE: You work in a fast-food restaurant, right?

DARREN: Yeah, and the people I work with, they're all black and a bunch of ignorant dropouts. I mean, one guy can barely read. Making $6.55 an hour isn't much for me, but I'm living with my mom now, so it's just spending money. These people, though, it's like they're just stuck.

GIBBONS: Do you think your co-workers are really ignorant, or have they just made a series of bad life choices that landed them in a dead-end situation?

DARREN: Both. I mean, I can't be using big words or talking proper, or those guys I work with will be like, "Man, you're so fuckin' white."

The conversation generated by Darren's story about the way he talks to his co-workers provides a natural segue into a discussion of the language we use for communicating in various social contexts. Though I believe in respecting whatever language students choose to use in their everyday speech or in casual conversations, I know that I am doing them a huge disservice if I let them leave my classroom without a firm grasp of Standard English and the knowledge that they need to use it in their speech or writing, whenever it is appropriate. Discussions such as these reinforce the point I try to make all term: Issues of right or wrong aside, people draw conclusions about us based upon the way we speak.

One language extension activity students enjoy involves preparing a slang dictionary. Sometimes this is an assignment; other times it is an extra credit opportunity; but the requirements are always the same: compile ten or more slang terms that you use in everyday speech or that are esoteric to a hobby or interest of yours and present them in dictionary form, writing the definitions in Standard English. After the students complete their dictionaries and turn them in, they enjoy sharing their work and seeing what classmates have written. In this way, we celebrate elements of their teenage lives and culture while reinforcing key concepts about language usage.

Opening Mindsets through Dialogue

In her essay "Full Circle," Nichelle Tramble juxtaposes her high school experiences reading *To Kill a Mockingbird* in a class where the students rebelled against reading racial epithets aloud with her adult experiences as a writer striving to write dialogue that is true to her characters. Her reflections are especially applicable to classroom contexts, where we strive to create a forum for open mindedness and discussion:

> Pretending that a word, a word that has been classified as "bad," does not exist, or refusing to acknowledge it by crossing it out on a page, does not negate its existence. Neither does it negate the circumstances that led to its being "bad." Dialogue, real dialogue, about its origins and history, its significance in both the past and the present, is the only way to deal with it. A whispered word is an empowered word. My suggestion is that we strip these words of their power, force them to lose their clout, and not allow them to be used as weaponry. (39)

Clearly, as teachers we must moderate these types of discussions closely, for they can become emotionally charged and volatile as students speak from their heart and collective life experiences. However, these discussions need to take place.

Help, If You Need It

Although it is impossible for us to anticipate every challenge, it helps to know our students and community, secure administrative support for our curriculum, and keep written rationales on file. Clearly, our role as educators includes the responsibility for expanding students' perspectives and fostering acceptance for diversity, but as classroom teachers, we must be in tune with the pervasive values and beliefs in a school community and remain aware that sometimes our curricular choices will challenge firmly entrenched belief systems. This can be challenging for veteran teachers who have taught in a community for many years, but achieving this degree of awareness poses a tremendous hurdle for novice teachers who are new to a school setting. For these reasons, novice teachers can benefit from the insight their department chairperson or another mentor teacher will be able to offer regarding the type of reception a particular text might receive. By no means am I suggesting that any teacher allow others to dictate the works included in the curriculum; rather, I am offering the suggestion that preparedness involves familiarizing oneself with the terrain before forging ahead, whenever possible.

The National Council of Teachers of English (NCTE) provides educators with assistance through their anticensorship website, which can be accessed at http://www.ncte.org. A search for "censorship" will lead to numerous resources, including the procedure for reporting a censorship incident. Support is there if you need it.

6 Responding to Criticism and Primary Documents

▪ ▪

Sometimes students who have not been exposed to literary criticism will draw the logical conclusion that "criticism" refers to negative comments about an author's work rather than to an analysis of the piece. Yet the broader and more diverse perspectives literary criticism offers challenge students to use their higher-order thinking skills as they synthesize their own opinions with those of the critics.

Additionally, because most literature reflects the sociocultural context in which it was written, students' understanding of a work is enhanced when they have some knowledge of related events that occurred at the time the author wrote the novel as well as other historical events alluded to or referenced in the work. For example, knowing about the Great Depression will help students grasp the setting and characters' mindsets in *To Kill a Mockingbird*. For these reasons, incorporating activities that require students to read and respond to literary criticism or to primary sources is class time well spent that enhances their reading experience as well as prepares them for the challenges of college level course work.

Reviews Following *To Kill a Mockingbird*'s Initial Publication

Perhaps one of the novel's most unique characteristics is its point of view, with the adult Scout reminiscing about pivotal events in her formative years. Because the novel is a bildungsroman, this point of view works especially well, yet it poses some technical challenges for the author, because the narrator can relate only what the young Scout learns or experiences firsthand.

Phoebe Adams

Although Phoebe Adams concludes her review with mixed praise for *To Kill a Mockingbird* as "pleasant, undemanding reading," the majority of her review focuses on what she perceives as shortcomings in the novel's narrative structure:

> *To Kill a Mockingbird* . . . is frankly and completely impossible, being told in the first person by a six-year-old girl with the prose style of a well-educated adult. Miss Lee has, to be sure, made an attempt to confine the information in the text to what Scout would actually know, but it is no more than a causal gesture toward plausibility. . . . The surface of the story is an Alcottish filigree of games, mischief, squabbles with an older brother, troubles at school, and the like. None of it is painful, for Scout and Jem are happy children, brought up with angelic cleverness by their father and his old Negro housekeeper. Nothing fazes them much or long. Even the new first-grade teacher, a devotee of the "Dewey-decimal system" who is outraged to discover that Scout can already read and write, proves endurable in the long run.
>
> A variety of adults, mostly eccentric in Scout's judgment,

and a continual babble of incident make *To Kill a Mockingbird* pleasant, undemanding reading.

Adams, Phoebe. "The *Atlantic* Bookshelf: Reader's Choice." Rev. of *To Kill a Mockingbird*, by Harper Lee. *Atlantic Monthly* 206 (August 1960): 98–99.

Edgar Schuster

In another one of the novel's initial reviews, educator Edgar Schuster focuses on the enlightenment that comes from learning what people are really like, an experience that mirrors dominant themes in the novel.

> The achievement of Harper Lee is not that she has written another novel about race prejudice, but rather that she has placed race prejudice in a perspective which allows us to see it as an aspect of a larger thing, as something that arises from phantom contacts, from fear and lack of knowledge; and finally as something that disappears with the kind of knowledge or "education" that one gains through learning what people are like when you "finally see them."

Schuster, Edgar H. "Discovering Theme and Structure in the Novel" *English Journal* 52.7 (October 1963): 506–511. 22 June 2008 <http://www.jstor.org/stable/810774>.

The Pulitzer Prize

Many works that hold a secure place in the literary canon have won prestigious awards and recognition, but students need assistance in forging connections between the work itself and the criteria for receiving a specific award. For this reason, some background information on the Pulitzer Prize helps students recognize the sociohistorical relevance that *To Kill a Mockingbird* has to the events of the 1960s.

Recognized as one of the highest honors a work of journalism, literature, or music can receive, the Pulitzer Prize is awarded annually in twenty-one categories. Administered by Columbia University, the institution whose journalism school was originally funded by Joseph Pulitzer, the prize carries with it a certificate, a cash award of ten thousand dollars, and priceless professional recognition for the recipient. In the fiction category, the prize is awarded to a distinguished work by an American author, preferably a text dealing with American life.

Growing up as the daughter of *Monroe Journal* editor and owner Amasa Lee and writing for a campus humor magazine during her college years, Harper Lee would have had firsthand knowledge of current social issues as well as familiarity with reporting methods. Even more important, as a native southerner, Lee would have viewed events of the late 1950s through the lens of her lifelong experiences living in an antiquated social system and would have recognized the stirrings of societal change, harbingers of the Civil Rights Movement of the 1960s.

Art Imitating Life
Buford Boone

Ever since *To Kill a Mockingbird*'s 1960 publication, critics and readers alike have sought parallels between characters and events in the novel and those from Lee's own realm of experience. Through the years, Lee has maintained that her book is a work of fiction, but one similarity of many that emerges is in the tone of the editorial written by Braxton Bragg Underwood, editor and publisher of the *Maycomb Tribune*, and those of Buford Boone, editor and publisher of *The Tuscaloosa News* from 1947 to 1968, whose editorials calling for calm and tolerance in the aftermath of an African American student's admittance into the University of Alabama earned him the 1957 Pulitzer Prize for Editorial Writing. Regardless of whether B. B. Underwood is based on the real life Buford Boone, reading Boone's editorial "What a Price for Peace" enhances students' understanding of the social climate in which Lee was writing *To Kill a Mockingbird*:

> When mobs start imposing their frenzied will on universities, we have a bad situation.
>
> But that is what has happened at the University of Alabama. And it is a development over which the community of Tuscaloosa should be deeply ashamed—and more than a little afraid.
>
> Our government's authority springs from the will of the people. But their wishes, if we are to be guided by democratic processes, must be expressed by ballot at the polls, by action in the legislative halls, and finally by interpretation from the bench. No intelligent expression ever has come from a crazed mob, and it never will.
>
> And make no mistake. There was a mob, in the worst sense, at the University of Alabama yesterday.
>
> Every person who witnessed the events there with comparative detachment speaks of the tragic nearness with which our great University came to being associated with murder—yes, we said murder.
>
> "If they could have gotten their hands on her, they would have killed her."

That was the considered judgment, often expressed, of the many who watched the action without participating in it.

The target was Authurine Lucy. Her "crimes"? She was born black, and she was moving against Southern custom and tradition—but with the law, right on up to the United States Supreme Court, on her side.

What does it mean today at the University of Alabama, and here in Tuscaloosa, to have the law on your side?

The answer has to be: Nothing—that is, if a mob disagrees with you and the courts.

As matters now stand, the University administration and trustees have knuckled under to the pressures and desires of the mob. What is to keep the same mob, if uncontrolled again, from taking over in any other field where it decides to impose its wishes? Apparently, nothing.

What is the answer to a mob? We think that is clear. It lies in firm, decisive action. It lies in the use of whatever force is necessary to restrain and subdue anyone who is violating the law.

Not a single University student has been arrested on the campus and that is no indictment against the men in uniform, but against higher levels which failed to give them clear-cut authority to go along with responsibility.

What has happened here is far more important than whether a Negro girl is admitted to the University. We have a breakdown of law and order, an abject surrender to what is expedient rather than a courageous stand for what is right.

Yes, there's peace on the University campus this morning. But what a price has been paid for it!

Boone, Buford. "What a Price for Peace." Editorial. *Tuscaloosa News* 7 Feb. 1956.

Although an in-depth discussion of the Pulitzer Prize is beyond the scope of this work, teachers and students can use resources offered on the Pulitzer organization's excellent website, www. Pulitzer.org, including a history of the prize, an archive of past winners, and a searchable database.

■ ■ ■ ■ ■ ■ ■ ■ ■ ■ ■ ■ ■ ■ ■ ■

The Novel as a Bildungsroman
Kathyrn Lee Seidel

In her essay "Growing Up Southern: Resisting the Code for Southerners in *To Kill a Mockingbird*," Kathryn Lee Seidel discusses Scout's maturation as it reflects a divergence from undesirable traits of the status quo:

> Scout embodies all the faults of the Old South when we first meet her. She is prone to violence; she fights for apparently no reason other than her honor and her own amusement. She is an elitist. She labels people according to their social class, denigrates them, and justifies her mistreatment of them because of what she perceives to be their genetic tendency for inferior behavior. She uses racist language, for example, asking Atticus, "Do you defend niggers . . . ?" (82). She is prejudiced against all manner of persons, including African Americans and people of lower social classes. She believes in and is a practitioner of the code of honor rather than the rule of law; it is this code that leads her to punch her cousin when he insults her (92).

The novel is indeed a bildungsroman in which Scout must grow from innocence to maturity, but her innocence is sharply defined by tendencies which if developed could lead her to becoming the worst type of southerner with the worst prejudices and behaviors—a member of a mob, rather than a member of the good. She must learn empathy (36) and compromise (38) and, as her father says, to fight "'with [her] head,'" not her fists (84). She must learn to respect African Americans and people from the lower classes. As Eric Sundquist points out, *Mockingbird* is very much a novel of its time, informed as much by *Brown vs. Board of Education* as by the Depression era of its setting. Sundquist asserts that the dawn of desegregation in the South allows Lee to prepare southerners for a revisioning as moving away from the traditional attitudes and becoming more wise, more tolerant (184). It is Scout who makes the journey that Lee is espousing, a journey from prejudice to tolerance, from ignorance to wisdom, from violence to self-control, from bigotry to empathy, from a code of honor to a code of law. (81)

Seidel, Kathryn Lee. "Growing Up Southern: Resisting the Code for Southerners in *To Kill a Mockingbird*." *On Harper Lee: Essays and Reflections*. Ed. Alice Hall Petry. Knoxville: University of Tennessee Press, 2007. 79–92.

The Title as Social Commentary
Jacqueline Tavernier-Courbin

Numerous discussions focus on the significance of the novel's title and the symbolism of the various mockingbirds, but critic

Jacqueline Tavernier-Courbin offers this perspective regarding ironic undertones of the mockingbird motif:

> A number of critics have discussed the novel's title, and while Calvin Woodard offers the most thorough examination of its relevance to the novel, he nevertheless does not take into account the belligerence of the little bird. Instead, he views the mockingbird largely as a symbol of tolerance because it identifies with, listens to, and learns from others; he sees it only as less than virtuous because it conforms too much to the will of others. This interpretation certainly does correspond with Lee's plea for tolerance but has little to do with humor. However, if one takes into account the mockingbird's aggressiveness, it then can become a symbol of hypocrisy rather than tolerance—pretending to be what it is not. Its emulating the songs of other birds would then link the mockingbird more closely to the "sickness" of intolerance and racism pervading the southern states, to the hypocrisy of the legal system merely going through the pretense of dispensing justice, and the mendacity of the missionary circle voicing Christian beliefs but contradicting them in action. Indeed, while the mockingbird is not the official state bird of Alabama, it is the state bird of five southern states and is generally seen as symbolizing the South.
>
> Its very name evocatively including the word "mocking" (imitating, but also ridiculing through imitation, and expressing scorn), the mockingbird could also symbolize the satirist revealing the ugly underbelly of the South through humor. Laughter kills by exposing the gangrene under the beautiful surface but also by demeaning it; one can hardly allow oneself to be controlled by what one is

able to laugh at. Thus those who laugh—i.e., those who are not taken in by pretenses but debunk the system and accepted norms—are not always popular with the powers that be, as the fate of many a satirist has witnessed throughout the centuries. Intolerance and fanaticism kill the "mockingbirds." However, satires and satirists have often been very popular with the reading public and have on occasion been known to be the instruments of change. This is the case with *To Kill a Mockingbird*. Thanks in large part to her skillful handling of humor, Harper Lee has created in her popular, unpretentious novel a still-powerful instrument for raising the level of consciousness about the effects of racism in the South. (59)

Tavernier-Courbin, Jacqueline. "Humor and Humanity in *To Kill a Mockingbird*." *On Harper Lee: Essays and Reflections*. Ed. Alice Hall Petry. Knoxville: University of Tennessee Press, 2007. 41–60.

The Novel as a 1960s Text
Gerald Early

In the excerpt that follows, Gerald Early reflects on the novel's southern gothic elements that reflect the nation's growth during the turbulent 1960s:

No geographical location more haunts the American mind and soul than the South. Our bloodiest battles involved the South: first, the Civil War, which ended chattel slavery in the United States, the first "peculiar" southern institution (although by no means purely southern, as, at one time, the entire country had slavery, and everyone, whether in slave or free states, continued to believe in white supremacy), and then the Civil Rights Movement, which ended racial segregation in the United States, a second "peculiar" southern institution that was practiced in the rest of the country in less blatantly psychotic ways. In its most memorable phase, from 1955 to 1965, the Civil Rights Movement took place largely on southern streets in the form of pitched expressions of violence, no less intense than the Civil War, between pacific demonstrators on the one side and hostile police and white townspeople on the other. The race war against Indians and their subsequent subjugation were terrible but not central to our sense of ourselves as Americans because, in the end, we did not truly have to live with Indians or seriously deal with their presence as a force in defining our society. We Americans simply eliminated them. On the other hand, the subjugation of blacks and the race war that was fought against them from the era of Reconstruction to Birmingham and Selma in the 1960s, when they insisted on full citizenship, were central to our national identity because non-black Americans did live with and among them—and because, while they could be terrorized, they could not be eliminated. Blacks came to define the nature of our democracy and our social customs by their presence. Our political system was found to be in crisis on more than one occasion because of them and the difficulty associated with their status. Since so much of this drama was played out either in the South or through the agency of the South or in conflict with the beliefs of the South (both political and theological), and since so much of our national identity involves what nonsoutherners do and do not share, historically, with the South, our anguished American soul is much like Boo Radley in Harper Lee's famous southern novel, *To Kill a Mockingbird* (1960). He is the strange Doppelgänger of the national conscience, a madman trapped inside our haunted house, the ghost (why else call him "Boo"?) not only of the middle-class southern liberal Atticus Finch (the good father), but also of the rabid, lower-class racist, Bob Ewell (the bad father); and it is the conflict between these two men that is the basis of this book. Radley, who may seem nothing more than a parody of a Gothic-novel type, is neither of these men, yet his goodness and individuality are the shadows of Atticus, just as his isolation and violence are the shadows of Ewell. *To Kill a Mockingbird*, arguably the most popular novel written by a southerner about the South—I am not convinced it has dethroned Margaret Mitchell's *Gone with the Wind* (1936)—seems a tale that gives us not a single story merely (which it does) but encounters of various narrative dimensions with various institutions: the family, the school, the church, the court, the prisons, all the institutions that, in some way or another, define human life or, more precisely put, what makes us human. Lee's novel is not about how these institutions work or fail to work. Rather, it is about how the *way* they work makes the South "southern." For being southern (at least white and southern) involves learning to negotiate the tensions that threaten to tear apart the South while managing to keep it whole. (94–95)

Early, Gerald. "The Madness in the American Haunted House: The New Southern Gothic, and the Young Adult Novel of the 1960s: A Personal Reflection." *On Harper Lee: Essays and Reflections.* Ed. Alice Hall Petry. Knoxville: University of Tennessee Press, 2007. 93–103.

The Character of Atticus Finch: A Crusader for Social Justice or Simply a Skilled Attorney?

Besides the reviews focusing on historical and literary aspects of *To Kill a Mockingbird*, a substantial body of work examines the novel's legal aspects, especially those pertaining to the character of Atticus Finch and his defense of Tom Robinson. Although the majority of writings glorify Atticus Finch as the quintessential crusader for social justice, a few legal experts have questioned the character's motives. Because of the dissenting yet fresh perspectives their voices offer, I have included two of them.

Steven Lubet

In the excerpt that follows, Northwestern University law professor Steven Lubet considers the circumstances of the trial and challenges readers to reexamine their impressions of Atticus by offering the premise that if Mayella Ewell was indeed telling the truth, Atticus would simply have been doing his job of defending his client, Tom Robinson. Lubet asks readers to reassess their opinion of Atticus after considering whether Tom Robinson was telling the truth, or he was lying, or a third possibility:

> . . . in reality perhaps the most likely one, is that Atticus did not care about the relative truth of the charge and defense. He was appointed by the court to defend Tom Robinson, an obligation that he could not ethically decline or shirk. Atticus Finch was neither a firebrand nor a reformer. He had spent his career hoping to avoid a case like Tom's, but having been given one, he was determined to do his best for his client. Not every Maycomb lawyer would have done as much.
>
> In the classic formulation, every person accused of a crime is entitled to a vigorous defense. Guilt or innocence

do not figure into the equation; that is for the jury to decide, not the attorney. It is not uncommon for lawyers to avoid learning, or forming strong convictions, about their clients' guilt, since zealous advocacy is required in either case.

Agnostic lawyers take their clients as they find them, assigning to themselves the task of assembling the most persuasive possible defense supported by the facts of the case. Their goal is to create a reasonable doubt in the mind of at least one juror, not to prove the innocence of the client. Innocence is irrelevant. Doubt is all that matters.

Doubt, in turn, may be found only in the mind of the beholder. A case is not tried in the abstract, but rather to a very specific audience. It is the lawyer's job—the advocate's duty—to identify and address the sensibilities, predispositions, insecurities, and thought patterns of the jury. Following this model, Atticus Finch defended Tom Robinson neither in the name of truth nor in disregard of it. He defended Tom Robinson in a way that he hoped might work. (1349–1350)

Atticus Finch, a pillar of the Maycomb establishment, mistrusted Mayella Ewell and believed Tom Robinson. In the Alabama of 1935, or even 1960, that was no small achievement. The "code" of his time and place required that a white woman's word always be accepted and that a black man was never to be trusted. Atticus was not a civil rights crusader, but he was able to look past race in structuring his defense. He was even optimistic that the jurors might see the light and agree with him. Surely there had been other racial injustices in Maycomb, but we have no hint that any prior incident had ever stirred Atticus to action. He was, if anything, indulgent of the tendency to prejudice, and almost amused by the Ku Klux Klan. What was special about the prosecution of Tom Robinson? What was it that enabled Atticus Finch to take his worthy stand?

Perhaps the time was right. Perhaps, upon appointment by the court, his duty was simply clear. And perhaps the social structure of Maycomb actually depended upon the humiliation of Mayella Ewell, even while it required the conviction of Tom Robinson. The Ewells, after all, were a disappointment to their race. Social outcasts, they were drunk, illiterate, filthy, welfare-dependent, and worse. Tom Robinson, on the other hand, was a "respectable Negro," polite, hard working, and not a trouble-maker. (1359–1360)

Mayella and her father, though, were just the opposite. They broke the mold, insulted the norms, violated the rules and the culture. They were the very contradiction of everything that the "fine folks" of Maycomb stood for. If Tom Robinson never caused a "speck o' trouble," the Ewells were pure trouble.

Can there be any doubt that this unexpected role reversal—the proper Negro versus the offensive whites—allowed Atticus Finch, and to a lesser extent even the sheriff (and perhaps even the judge and the prosecutor), to see class, perhaps for the first time, as a more salient characteristic than race? Of course, in the Alabama of 1935, race could not be dismissed. Innocent or guilty, Tom Robinson had to pay the price for allowing himself to get into an unforgivable predicament. But neither could class or gender be overlooked. As surely as Tom had to be convicted, Mayella Ewell, again, innocent or guilty, had to be disgraced.

Where does this leave us, and what do we think now of Atticus Finch? At the very least we must renew our respect for his skill as an advocate. It is a great accomplishment, of course, to compel a bigoted Alabama jury to hesitate before convicting an innocent black man. But it would take a monumental performance indeed to accomplish that same feat for a guilty defendant. On a purely technical level, it is safe to say that Atticus remains an icon, if not an idol.

The moral problem is more difficult, if not intractable. Whether Tom was innocent or guilty, Atticus no doubt fulfilled his obligations under the standard conception of professional ethics. But that only brings us directly to the hardest question of all: Is Atticus still a hero? Does his moral standing depend on Tom's innocence, or can we still idealize him if it turns out that Tom committed the crime? If Atticus knew, or ignored the possibility, of Tom's guilt, does that reduce him in our eyes to a talented, but, shall we say, morally neutral actor? (1361)

Lubet, Steven. "Reconstructing Atticus Finch." *Michigan Law Review* 97.6 (May 1999): 1339–1362.

▪▪▪▪▪▪▪▪▪▪▪▪▪▪▪▪

Monroe Freedman

Not only has Atticus Finch achieved iconic status in literary circles, but he holds a prominent position in the legal world as well. For example, in 1997 the Alabama Bar Association placed a commemorative monument honoring Atticus in the Courthouse Square in Monroeville, the first of this sort in the state's history. Not surprisingly, Monroe Freedman's article "Atticus Finch, Esq., R.I.P." sparked a flurry of controversy in the legal world, with numerous attorneys rushing to Atticus's defense. In the article Freedman criticizes Atticus Finch's status as a role model for lawyers on the basis that Atticus is appointed to defend Tom Robinson—he does not volunteer to take the case—and, Freedman argues, his risking his life to stand down a lynch mob is not the sort of thing attorneys need to be prepared to do. Additionally, Freedman points out that Atticus's status as a "gentleman" suggests exclusivity, and indeed Atticus lives comfortably in a segregated society, so Freedman concludes with the idea that Atticus's defense of Tom Robinson stems from an innate sense of noblesse oblige:

> Atticus Finch does, indeed, act heroically in his represen-tation of Robinson. But he does so from an elitist sense of noblesse oblige. Except under compulsion of a court ap-pointment, Finch never attempts to change the racism and sexism that permeate the life of Macomb [sic], Ala. On the contrary, he lives his own life as the passive participant in that pervasive injustice. And that is not my idea of a role model for young lawyers.
>
> Let me put it this way. I would have more respect for Atticus Finch if he had never been compelled by the court to represent Robinson, but if, instead, he had undertaken voluntarily to establish the right of the black citizens of Macomb [sic] to sit freely in their county courthouse. That Atticus Finch would, indeed, have been a model for young lawyers to emulate.
>
> Don't misunderstand, I'm not saying that I would pres-ent as role models those truly admirable lawyers who, at great personal sacrifice, have dedicated their entire professional lives to fighting for social injustice. That's too easy to preach and too hard to practice.

Rather, the lawyers we should hold up as role models are those who earn their living in the kinds of practices that most lawyers pursue—corporate, trusts and estates, litigation, even teaching—but who also volunteer a small but significant amount of their time and skills to advance social justice. That is the cause that Atticus Finch, a gentleman of character, chose to ignore throughout his legal career.

Freedman, Monroe. "Atticus Finch, Esq., R.I.P." *Legal Times* 24 Feb. 1992: 20–21.

Response Activities

The prompts that follow encourage students to reflect on the preceding literary criticism and primary documents and can be used to stimulate reading, writing, and discussion in a variety of contexts.

- Describe recent court cases in which the attorneys involved received as much or more attention than the circumstances of the case itself.

- Discuss one or more event—either in American history or in the larger global society—that has prompted mob violence. What were the results?

- Lee employs a unique narrative structure throughout *To Kill a Mockingbird*, with the adult Scout recounting events from her childhood. Explain why you agree or disagree with critic Phoebe Adams's dismissal of Lee's narrative style as "impossible."

- In the years following *To Kill a Mockingbird*'s publication, Atticus Finch has become larger in the eyes of an adoring public than he is in the pages of the novel. Describe a public figure, either living or dead, who is idolized because of his or her virtuous traits or actions.

■ Schuster writes that racial prejudice "arises from phantom contacts, from fear and lack of knowledge" but "disappears with the kind of knowledge or 'education' that one gains through learning what people are like when you 'finally see them.'" Recount a personal experience or one of a national or global scope that illustrates Schuster's perspective.

■ Seidel's criticism focuses on Scout as the embodiment of the Old South metamorphosing into the New South. Consider other characters in more contemporary novels you have read and discuss ways that the protagonist or another character reflects life in twenty-first century American society.

Additional Resources

JOHNSON, CLAUDIA D. To Kill a Mockingbird: *Threatening Boundaries.* Twayne's Masterwork Studies, No. 139. New York: Twayne Publishers, 1994.

Though written from a scholarly perspective, Johnson's comprehensive analysis of the novel is easy to read and offers background and criticism that teachers will find helpful.

————. *Understanding* To Kill a Mockingbird: *A Student Casebook to Issues, Sources, and Historic Documents.* The Greenwood Press "Literature in Context" Series. Westport, CT: Greenwood Press, 1994.

A companion piece to Johnson's *Threatening Boundaries,* this text includes numerous primary documents as well as study questions and teaching ideas.

MOATES, MARIANNE M. *A Bridge of Childhood: Truman Capote's Southern Years.* New York: Henry Holt, 1989.

This collection of stories the author gleaned from interviews with Jennings Faulk Carter (cousin and childhood friend of Capote) recounts events from the summers Capote, Lee, and Carter spent together. Many of the stories parallel events depicted in *To Kill a Mockingbird*.

SHIELDS, CHARLES J. *Mockingbird: A Portrait of Harper Lee*. New York: Henry Holt, 2006.

In the introduction, Shields states that Harper Lee refused numerous requests for her input into the manuscript. But even though this book is an unauthorized biography, it remains an informative work that provides insight into Harper Lee's life and her career.

7 *To Kill a Mockingbird*: The Film

■ ■

Harper Lee and Foote reach deep into the collective unconsciousness of Americans that gives *Huck Finn* so much of its emotional appeal and retell the story of childhood—the adventures of preadolescents, the excitement, and the danger. The story has the universal appeal of gripping childhood experience, occurring some thirty years ago. Foote did not tamper with that strain but enriched it by putting into visual form—what the novel could not—the children's view of their mysterious neighbor and their confrontations with life and death in the adult world. (145)

—from *Horton Foote: A Literary Biography* by Charles S. Watson

Reviews of *To Kill a Mockingbird* as a film

Time *Magazine*

If we consider Norman Mailer's opinion that great novels make the most disappointing movies, the film version of *To Kill a Mockingbird* emerges as something of an anomaly. Directed by Robert Mulligan and produced by Alan Pakula, the 1962 film received favorable reviews, as the following excerpt from the movie's February 22, 1963, review in *Time* illustrates:

> In her famous first novel, which won the Pulitzer Prize for 1960, Harper Lee found quite as much to fear as she found to love in Maycomb County—and by Maycomb County she

obviously meant the South. Of what she was fearful, she framed an Alabama melodrama that etched its issues in black and white. Of what was lovable, on the other hand, she made a tomboy poem as full of hick fun as *Huck Finn*, a sensitive feminine testament to the Great American Childhood. In this film Director Robert Mulligan and Scenarist Horton Foote have translated both testament and melodrama into one of the year's most fetching and affecting pictures. (93)

"Boo Radley Comes Out." *Time* 22 Feb. 1963: 93.

■ ■ ■ ■ ■ ■ ■ ■ ■ ■ ■ ■ ■ ■ ■ ■

Bosley Crowther

Perhaps the most marked difference between the novel and the film is the shift in focus: while the novel focuses on ways that Scout and Jem mature as a result of events related to the Tom Robinson trial, the movie centers on Atticus and his role as a promoter of social justice. For example, the following excerpt from Bosley Crowther's *New York Times* review praises the movie, but notes the void this change in perspective creates:

> There is so much feeling for children in the film that has been made from Harper Lee's best-selling novel, *To Kill a Mockingbird*[,] . . . so much delightful observation of their spirit, energy, and charm as depicted by two superb discoveries, Mary Badham and Phillip Alford—that it is a bit of a letdown at the end to realize that, for all the picture's feeling for children, it doesn't tell us very much of how they feel.
>
> This is the one adult omission that is regretful in this fine film that Alan J. Pakula and Universal delivered to the Music Hall yesterday.

Crowther, Bosley. "Screen: 'To Kill a Mockingbird'" Rev. of *To Kill a Mockingbird*, dir. by Robert Mulligan. Special to *New York Times* 15 Feb. 1963. Accessed through ProQuest Historical Newspapers. *New York Times with Index* (1851–2005).

Despite these changes, Harper Lee's comments on the film reflect her overall approval: "If the integrity of a film adaptation is measured by the degree to which the novelist's intent is preserved, Mr. Foote's screenplay should be studied as a classic" (Foote, back cover). Ultimately, the film scored eight Oscar nominations and won in the following three categories: Best Actor (Gregory Peck); Best Adapted Screenplay (Horton Foote); and Best Art and Set Direction (Alexander Golitzen, Henry Bumstead, and Oliver Emert).

With the film's Oscar wins now almost a half-century in the past, the retrospective focus the passage of years provides makes it easy to see how in the midst of the synchronous turmoil and optimism that shaped American society in the early 1960s, *To Kill a Mockingbird* was the right film at the right time. And Gregory Peck, with an established reputation as a virtuous on-screen presence, was the right actor in the right role, a performance he referred to as the highlight of his career. Additionally, like the novel, the film has staying power, moving from its place as number 24 on the American Film Institute's 1998 ranking of the "100 Best American Films of All-Time" to number 25 on the Institute's 2007 list.

Thomas Mallon

Just as a large body of criticism focuses on the novel, numerous articles focus on the film as well, and more than forty years following the film's initial release, the publication of Charles F. Shields's biography *Mockingbird: A Portrait of Harper Lee* prompted Thomas

Mallon to reflect on the film, which he feels is "rather better than the original material" [the book itself]. Mallon explains:

> Lee's agents handled the book with care, getting it into the sensitive hands of the director Robert Mulligan and the producer Alan J. Pakula. To play Atticus, Lee wanted Spencer Tracy and Universal wanted Rock Hudson; Bing Crosby wanted himself. The part went to Gregory Peck. . . .
>
> Peck's performance is top-heavy with a kind of civic responsibility, and a Yankee frost often kills his carefully tended Southern accent, but his Atticus is still more subtle than the book's. Credit here must go to Horton Foote's screenplay, which, unlike most Hollywood adaptations, tends to prune rather than gild the dialogue from its published source. In the book, Scout asks Atticus if he really is a "nigger-lover," as she's heard him called, and he responds, "I certainly am. I do my best to love everybody." Foote skips this cloying exchange, and has the father explain himself with a less self-regarding line from the book: "I'm simply defending a Negro." The same principle of selection is at work when it comes to Jem's exasperation with his sister. Foote uses a close variant of a plain line from Lee ("I swear, Scout, you act more like a girl all the time"), rather than the archly impossible line ("You act so much like a girl it's mortifyin'") that she also makes available.
>
> The novel is full of set pieces that provide either local color or the opportunity for some Aesopian underlining of Atticus's rectitude. Mulligan filmed and then cut an episode in which Mrs. Dubose, a local termagant, is shown trying to free herself from a secret morphine habit before she dies. Good as the actress Ruth White's performance of the scene

was, "it stopped the film," Pakula realized. The episode stops the novel, too, but provides Atticus with the chance to make a speech about courage ("She was the bravest person I ever knew"). Lubricated with the syrup of Elmer Bernstein's score, the movie has a propulsion that the novel never achieves. The film even solves the book's vocal problems, extracting bits of the adult narrative to use, sparingly, as voice-over.

Mallon, Thomas. "The Critics—Books—Big Bird: A Biography of the Novelist Harper Lee." *The New Yorker* 29 May 2006: 79–82.

Teaching Films as Texts

Opinions vary widely among English language arts teachers as to whether film versions of literary works have any place in our curriculum: With so much to do teaching reading, grammar, writing, and literature, we must be able to justify decisions regarding the ways we allocate instructional time. However, just as some works of published writing warrant close reading and analysis more than others, some films deserve our attention as well, and the film version of *To Kill a Mockingbird* is one such work. Students will benefit from watching all or portions of the film, because the film is a text separate from the original novel: it represents a screenwriter's and director's interpretations, presented through the collaborative efforts of actors and technicians, that are captured using the medium of film. Additionally, just as we discuss the role of revision in the writing process, a comparison of the film's opening scene and Foote's final screenplay (excerpted in Chapter 3) reveals that a parallel process takes place during movie production.

Although various scheduling configurations govern our teaching situations, analytical and comparative activities related to viewing all or part of the movie version of *To Kill a Mockingbird* complement a class study of the novel. I teach on a ninety-six-minute block schedule, which I try to divide into three, approximately thirty-minute-long instructional activities in an effort to keep students engaged, since attention spans wane quickly. I've found that showing a clip of the movie at the beginning or middle of class, accompanied by a specific instructional goal or task, enhances our study of the text.

However, whenever I assign a writing prompt or give students a viewing guide to complete as they watch, many students respond with groans, complaining that completing the assigned activity will distract them and interrupt their viewing. But as teachers, we must help students understand differences separating home and academic environments. Just as the process of reading a popular paperback novel on the beach during our vacation differs from the type of reading and analysis we do for academic reading, contexts for viewing differ from one setting to another as well. Because a generation of students who have grown up—literally—in front of the television tend to be passive viewers and see movie viewing as a time to relax rather than to think critically, we must help them understand that watching a film in the classroom is a different experience than leisurely viewing it at home. Just as they do with a text, viewing prompts for writing and discussion help focus students' attention on significant parts of the film and enable them to forge connections with their own experiences. For these reasons, we begin the movie with students responding to the following prompts, then sharing their ideas:

Revisiting Childhood:
The adult Scout narrates the novel, telling about events that happened during the three-year period when she was six to nine years old. Consider significant events from years past

and describe the type of movie you would make about your own childhood.

When the writing stops, students share reflections that range from fond reminiscences of times with friends to painful memories of domestic turmoil caused by divorce or the death of a parent or caregiver. Always, though, I am impressed by the mature insight reflected in students' themes of childhood, for in the relatively short amount of time they have been alive, they already have surmised that youth breeds a spirit of confidence and optimism bordering on invincibility; that life is one long process of change and starting over; and despite all the changes life brings, their childhood friends will be their friends for life.

Analyzing the Film's Opening Credits

Just as beginning a new novel involves looking at the cover art and skimming the text on the back of the book, the following prompt asks students to examine the movie's opening credits.

Prompt:
Watch closely as the opening credits appear on the screen, with a child's humming and single piano notes providing the only background music. Notice the various objects that appear as well, all of which hold significance in the novel. Describe the mood the visual and auditory imagery create for you, the viewer.

Cynthia's Response

As students read what they wrote, Cynthia's response reflects her grasp of the symbolism in the film's opening:

The simple music and child's humming create a feeling of simplicity and echo the sort of joy you only have when you're a kid. All of the objects are significant in the novel, but several hold special symbolism. For example, the ticking pocket watch symbolizes the passage of time and the changes that are coming to Maycomb's society. Also, the way the background music begins after the white marble hits the black marble reflects a sort of harmony that came after the racial conflict had died down. Finally, when the child tears up the crayon drawing, it symbolizes the end of childhood innocence and society's insensitive treatment of the novel's two "mockingbird" characters, Tom Robinson and Boo Radley.

Examining Southern Gothic Elements

Just as authors use literary techniques and plot devices to convey a story to their readers, directors rely on cinematic techniques to achieve their goals. Even though students are veteran viewers and consumers of a variety of media, they will benefit from focusing activities. For example, before beginning the movie, we review elements of southern gothic literature, in particular as these characteristics relate to the voice of the child narrator, a youngster who can be frightened easily. To help establish the naïveté of the narrator as well as to contrast today's world with the society of the 1930s, students write a brief response to the following question: in today's world, what do we fear? When the discussion begins, the students offer the following opinions:

CYNTHIA: Since Americans care more about money than anything else, this country's biggest fear is being poor. Everything America does is motivated by greed and selfishness, and everyone is fixated on how to make more money. It doesn't have anything to do with having your basic needs provided for; it's about superficial and material things.

HALEY: Yeah, I agree with Cynthia because everyone's life seems to revolve around wealth and making it into a higher social class. I don't think we could survive another Great Depression because we're used to having everything too easy, and even the wealthiest people have a lot of material possessions but not land where they could grow their own food if things got really bad.

GIBBONS: Both of you make good points. Do we have other opinions?

WILLIAM: Well, this is really obvious, but we fear the threat of terrorism. I mean, the 9/11 attacks changed life as we know it, and now we live with it as a constant threat.

TRENT: But I think what we fear goes beyond just the terrorism issue; it's more like a fear of all the things that are unknown to us—like we fear terrorism because we never know how or where an attack will happen, and we don't understand the mindsets of fanatic terrorists.

Clearly, one commonality emerges from the students' discussion: many intangible concerns that people of the past felt were lurking in the shadows—a general fear of change and the unknown—have become concrete realities that pose very real threats in today's world.

By the time we begin viewing the film version of *To Kill a Mockingbird*, students already have been introduced to gothic elements in literature, specifically in short stories of the southern gothic genre such as Flannery O'Connor's "A Good Man Is Hard to Find" and William Faulkner's "A Rose for Emily." We use the following definition as we examine elements of the genre in various literary works:

> **Southern gothic:** A subgenre of the gothic genre; a type of literature that relies on supernatural or unusual elements to propel the plot. Unlike gothic literature, southern gothic works use the supernatural or other unusual events to explore social issues and reveal characteristics of the American South.

Gothic elements in the novel, including the much maligned Boo Radley and the innately evil Bob Ewell, assume more prominence in the film version, in which lighting, camera angles, and music set a dangerous, foreboding mood. Although I provide some specific focusing prompts at the beginning and the end of the movie, students are already adept at recognizing cinematic conventions on their own. For this reason, I give them an open-ended viewing guide to organize their notes as we watch parts of the movie. Later, their notes serve as reminders during discussions.

After Viewing the Entire Film
Once we finish watching the movie, these prompts provide a basis for follow-up and extension activities (Figure 7.1):

- Describe how costumes are used to convey information about various characters. For example, consider Atticus, Mr. Cunningham, Walter Cunningham, Scout and Jem, Miss Maudie, and Calpurnia.

- Choose a scene from the book to compare to its counterpart in the movie. How are the two scenes similar and how are they different? What techniques does the filmmaker employ to convey the author's message?

List examples of southern gothic elements.	
List examples of how the novel's narrative structure (an adult Scout telling a story about something that happened during her childhood) is shown in the movie.	
List examples of how the camera shows the viewer the action through a child's eyes, those of young Scout, the narrator. (Consider camera angles, lighting, props, etc.)	
List examples of how Boo Radley's reputation is built up throughout the film.	
List examples of how the actors' demeanor, actions, and appearance enable them to fully develop the following characters: Atticus Finch (Gregory Peck), Scout Finch (Mary Badham), Bob Ewell (James Anderson), Mayella Ewell (Collin Wilcox), Tom Robinson (Brock Peters), and Boo Radley (Robert Duvall).	Atticus Finch
	Scout Finch
	Bob Ewell
	Mayella Ewell
	Tom Robinson
	Boo Radley
List effective examples of *mise en scène* (single camera shots that convey volumes of information, without dialogue).	

Figure 7.1. Viewing guide for *To Kill a Mockingbird*.

■ Some critics have suggested that the film is actually superior to the novel. Explain why you agree or disagree with this assessment and provide specific reasons and details to support your opinion.

Additional Resources
Audio and Video

Fearful Symmetry. Dir. Charles Kiselak. Universal Studios Home Video, 1998. (Running time = 90 minutes)

This in-depth documentary about making the movie is included on the collector's edition of the *To Kill a Mockingbird* DVD. Made up of interviews with filmmakers, cast, scholars, and Monroeville residents, as well as archival photographs and footage, the program focuses primarily on making the film. Additionally, it grounds the filmmaking in the social context of a bygone era as interviewees discuss changes that have occurred in Monroeville and in the South. Segments in which Monroeville residents reminisce about people and incidents that may have inspired characters and events in the novel are included. Teachers should preview this documentary, however, because photographs of lynched bodies and Ku Klux Klan rallies may be too disturbing to show in some classrooms.

In Context: To Kill a Mockingbird. BBC Production, 1997. VHS ISBN: 978-0-7365-1766-9; DVD ISBN: 978-0-7365-5755-9. (Running time = 20 minutes)

Filled with interviews, photographs, and archival footage, this video provides a frank discussion of segregation and racial issues in the South during the 1930s through the 1960s that will broaden students' understanding of the novel's sociohistorical context. Interviews with residents of Monroeville and photos of the area provide local color as well. Teachers should preview this carefully, however, because graphic photographs of a lynching are included.

An Introduction to To Kill a Mockingbird. National Endowment for the Arts. Written and directed by Dan Stone. 2006. (Running Time = 29 minutes)

This CD features excerpted readings from the novel as well as segments of commentary by David Baker, Robert Duvall, Horton Foote, Sandra Day O' Connor, Charles Shields, Curtis Sittenfeld, and Elizabeth Spencer.

The Song of the Mockingbird (Running time = 20 minutes)

An abbreviated program composed of segments from *Fearful Symmetry*, this documentary is included with some editions of the movie. In it director Robert Mulligan, producer Alan Pakula, screenwriter Horton Foote, and composer Elmer Bernstein discuss filming *To Kill a Mockingbird*. Students enjoy the interviews in which the actors discuss their role in making the picture. Segments with cast members Gregory Peck (Atticus), Phillip Alford (Jem), Mary Badham (Scout), Brock Peters (Tom), Collin Wilcox (Mayella), and Robert Duvall (Boo) are included.

To Kill a Mockingbird. Dir. Robert Mulligan. Perf. Gregory Peck, Mary Badham, Phillip Alford, John Megna, Ruth White, Paul Fix, Brock Peters, Frank Overton, Rosemary Murphy, and Collin Wilcox. Universal, 1962. Re-released, 1998. (Running time = 130 minutes)

Available in both VHS (ASIN: 0783222955) and DVD (ASIN: 0783225857), this re-release of the original 1962 film complements a class study of the novel.

Print Resources

COSTANZO, WILLIAM. *Great Films and How to Teach Them*. Urbana, IL: NCTE, 2004.

Costanzo offers sound ideas for integrating film study into the English language arts curriculum and provides resources that teachers will find helpful. Chapter 12 focuses entirely on the film *To Kill a Mockingbird*. In addition to a detailed analysis of the film, the chapter includes discussion questions, extension activities, and a list of specific scenes to analyze.

"*To Kill a Mockingbird*: Then and Now." *English Journal* 86.4 (1997): 1–16.

Originally published to supplement a 1997 teleconference event on the novel and the film, this teacher study guide offers background information on the novel as well as teaching resources. For those who cannot locate a back issue of *English Journal*, this resource is available for purchase through JSTOR: <http://www.jstor.org/stable/820996>.

Internet Sites

Film Study Guide for To Kill a Mockingbird: *Seeing the Film through the Lens of Media Literacy.* 1 July 2008 <http://www.frankwbakr.com/tkam1.htm>.

Media educator Frank Baker provides comprehensive Web resources related to teaching the film. With links to film reviews, teaching ideas, and a framework for analyzing the film, this website provides numerous resources.

Library of Congress. 28 Nov. 2008 <http://www.loc.gov/index.html>.

Searching "To Kill a Mockingbird" on the Library of Congress's website yields several excellent lesson plans, which include links to primary documents such as archival records and photographs from the American Memory Collection.

Monroe County Heritage Museums. 1 July 2008 <http://www.tokilla mockingbird.com/>.

Monroeville, Alabama, Harper Lee's hometown, offers resources that will benefit anyone interested in the novel. With walking tours, performances of a play-adaptation of the novel, and workshops for teachers, a visit to Monroeville offers a wealth of experiences related to the novel.

Chronology

1926 Nelle Harper Lee is born on April 28 in Monroe-ville, Alabama, to Amasa Coleman and Frances Finch Lee.

1928–1933 Lee's friend Truman Capote lives with Monroeville relatives next door to the Lee household.

1944–1945 Lee attends Huntingdon College, a private women's college in Montgomery, Alabama.

1945–1950 Lee transfers to the University of Alabama, where she writes for *Rammer-Jammer*, a campus humor magazine.

1947 Lee enrolls in the University of Alabama Law School and spends a term as an exchange student at Oxford University in England.

1950 Lee moves to New York City, where she holds various jobs, including reservations clerk for Eastern Air Lines and British Airways and bookstore clerk.

1951 Lee's mother, Frances Finch Lee, dies on June 2, and Lee's brother Edwin dies on June 12.

1956 Lee submits several short stories to literary agent Maurice Crain, who advises her to consider writing a novel. For Christmas Lee's friends give her a check, which allows her to quit working and devote all her time to writing.

1957   Lee meets with editors at J. B. Lippincott about her draft of *Atticus*, which Lee later retitles *To Kill a Mockingbird*.

1958   Lee completes the first draft of *To Kill a Mockingbird* and submits it to editor Tay Hohoff at J. B. Lippincott.

1959   With *To Kill a Mockingbird* complete and in press, Lee accompanies Truman Capote to Kansas to help research the Clutter family murder. Their research provides the basis of Capote's nonfiction novel *In Cold Blood*.

1960   *To Kill a Mockingbird* is published and selected by several book clubs. It becomes a *Reader's Digest* Condensed Book, a Literary Guild selection, and a Book-of-the-Month Club alternate.

1961   In April, *To Kill a Mockingbird* wins the Pulitzer Prize for literature. Lee's article "Love—in Other Words" appears in the April issue of *Vogue*. Robert Mulligan and Alan Pakula purchase the film rights to *To Kill a Mockingbird*. Lee's article "Christmas to Me" appears in the August issue of *McCall's*. In December, the novel wins the Brotherhood Award of the National Conference on Christians and Jews.

1962   Lee's father, Amasa Lee, dies on April 15. In May, Lee is awarded an honorary doctorate from Mount Holyoke College. Lee serves as a special consultant on the film based on her novel. The film *To Kill a*

Mockingbird premieres in December and receives eight Academy Award nominations. *To Kill a Mockingbird* wins the Paperback Bestseller's Award for the Year.

1964 A foreword by Harper Lee is included in the published version of Horton Foote's film script of *To Kill a Mockingbird.*

1966 President Lyndon B. Johnson appoints Harper Lee to the National Council on the Arts.

1970 Christopher Sergel dramatizes and publishes *To Kill a Mockingbird* as a full-length play.

1977 *To Kill a Mockingbird* is published in a special limited edition by Franklin Publications.

1982 *To Kill a Mockingbird* is published in a special limited edition by *Southern Living* magazine.

1983 Lee presents her essay "Romance and High Adventure" at the Alabama History and Heritage Festival in Eufaula, Alabama.

1990 The University of Alabama awards Lee an honorary doctorate. Monroeville, Alabama, begins staging the play based on the novel *To Kill a Mockingbird*, thirty years after its initial publication.

1997 Lee accepts an honorary doctorate from Spring Hill College in Mobile, Alabama.

1999 Librarians across America vote *To Kill a Mockingbird* the best novel of the twentieth century.

2001 Lee is inducted into the Alabama Academy of Honor. City officials in Chicago, Illinois, ask every adult and adolescent in the city to read *To Kill a Mockingbird* at the same time as part of their One City, One Book program.

2002   Perennial Classic publishes *To Kill a Mockingbird* in a trade paperback edition. New York City chooses *To Kill a Mockingbird* as the book for their citywide reading campaign.

2005   Lee is awarded the Los Angeles Public Library Literary Award.

2006   Lee attends an honorary dinner for Horton Foote at the Ritz-Carlton, New York. "A Letter from Harper Lee" is published in the July issue of *O: The Oprah Magazine.* Lee is awarded an honorary doctorate from the University of Notre Dame.

2007   Lee is awarded the Presidential Medal of Freedom, the nation's highest civilian award. Lee is inducted into the American Academy of Arts and Letters.

2008   *To Kill a Mockingbird* is number twenty-two on *USA Today*'s Best Selling Books list. Lee is inducted into the University of Alabama's College of Communications and Information Sciences Hall of Fame.

Works Cited

ADAMS, PHOEBE. "The *Atlantic* Bookshelf: Reader's Choice." Rev. of *To Kill a Mockingbird*, by Harper Lee. *Atlantic Monthly* 206 (August 1960): 98–99.

BOONE, BUFORD. "What a Price for Peace." Editorial. *Tuscaloosa News* 7 Feb. 1956.

"BOO RADLEY COMES OUT." *Time* 22 Feb. 1963: 93.

BURKE, JIM. "Developing Students' Textual Intelligence through Grammar." *Voices from the Middle* 8.3 (2001): 56–61.

CLARKE, GERALD. *Capote: A Biography.* New York: Ballantine Books, 1989.

CROWTHER, BOSLEY. "Screen: 'To Kill a Mockingbird'" Rev. of *To Kill a Mockingbird*, dir. by Robert Mulligan. Special to *New York Times* 15 Feb. 1963. Accessed through ProQuest Historical Newspapers. *New York Times with Index* (1851–2005).

EARLY, GERALD. "The Madness in the American Haunted House: The New Southern Gothic, and the Young Adult Novel of the 1960s: A Personal Reflection." *On Harper Lee: Essays and Reflections.* Ed. Alice Hall Petry. Knoxville: University of Tennessee Press, 2007. 93–103.

FOOTE, HORTON. To Kill a Mockingbird: *Final Screenplay / by Horton Foote.* Ts. 1919. Hoole Library Alabama Collection, U of Alabama Libraries, Tuscaloosa.

———. *Three Screenplays:* To Kill a Mockingbird, Tender Mercies, *and* The Trip to Bountiful. New York: Grove Press, 1994.

FREEDMAN, MONROE. "Atticus Finch, Esq., R.I.P." *Legal Times* 24 Feb. 1992: 20–21.

JOHNSON, CLAUDIA D. To Kill a Mockingbird: *Threatening Boundaries.* Twayne's Masterwork Studies, No. 139. New York: Twayne Publishers, 1994.

JOHNSON, RHETA GRIMSLEY. "The Legacy of Harper Lee: Isn't Writing One Classic Novel Enough?" *The Atlanta Constitution* 25 May 1993: A/11.

JONES, GEORGE THOMAS. "She Was the 'Queen of the Tomboys.'" *The Monroe Journal* 6 May 1999.

KING, STEPHEN. *On Writing: A Memoir of the Craft.* New York: Scribner, 2000.

LEE, HARPER. *To Kill a Mockingbird.* New York: Warner Books, 1960.

LUBET, STEVEN. "Reconstructing Atticus Finch." *Michigan Law Review* 97.6 (May 1999): 1339–62.

MALLON, THOMAS. "The Critics—Books—Big Bird: A Biography of the Novelist Harper Lee." *The New Yorker* 29 May 2006: 79–82.

MILLS, MARJA. "A Life Apart: Harper Lee, the Complex Woman behind 'a Delicious Mystery.'" *Chicago Tribune* 13 Sept. 2002: 1. 27 Jan. 2005 <http://www.chicagotribune.com/news/showcase/chi-0209130001sep13.story>.

MOATES, MARIANNE M. *A Bridge of Childhood: Truman Capote's Southern Years.* New York: H. Holt, 1989.

NODEN, HARRY R. *Image Grammar: Using Grammatical Structures to Teach Writing.* Portsmouth, NH: Heinemann, 1999.

RUDISILL, MARIE, AND JAMES C. SIMMONS. *The Southern Haunting of Truman Capote.* Nashville, TN: Cumberland House, 2000.

SCHUSTER, EDGAR H. "Discovering Theme and Structure in the Novel." *English Journal* 52.7 (October 1963): 506–511. 22 June 2008 <http://www.jstor.org/stable/810774>.

SEIDEL, KATHRYN LEE. "Growing Up Southern: Resisting the Code for Southerners in *To Kill a Mockingbird.*" *On Harper Lee: Essays and Reflections.* Ed. Alice Hall Petry. Knoxville: University of Tennessee Press, 2007. 79–92.

SHIELDS, CHARLES J. *Mockingbird: A Portrait of Harper Lee.* New York: Henry Holt, 2006.

TAVERNIER-COURBIN, JACQUELINE. "Humor and Humanity in *To Kill a Mockingbird.*" *On Harper Lee: Essays and Reflections.* Ed. Alice Hall Petry. Knoxville: University of Tennessee Press, 2007. 41–60.

TRAMBLE, NICHELLE D. "Full Circle: A Personal Reflection." *On Harper Lee: Essays and Reflections.* Ed. Alice Hall Petry. Knoxville: University of Tennessee Press, 2007. 35–40.

TRUSS, LYNNE. *Eats, Shoots & Leaves: The Zero Tolerance Approach to Punctuation.* New York: Gotham Books, 2004.

WATSON, CHARLES S. *Horton Foote: A Literary Biography.* The Jack and Doris Smothers Series in Texas History, Life, and Culture, No. 9. Austin: University of Texas Press, 2003.

WOLFE, TOM. "Interview with Laura Wilson." *I Am Charlotte Simmons.* North Kingstown, RI: Sound Library, 2004.

Author

Louel C. Gibbons teaches American literature and Advanced Placement literature and composition at Brookwood High School in Brookwood, Alabama. She also teaches courses for preservice teachers in the College of Education at the University of Alabama, Tuscaloosa. Her research interests include rhetorical grammar, reading and writing across the content areas, and secondary students' reading interests. She has presented teacher workshops on these topics and has coauthored articles that have appeared in the *Journal of Adolescent and Adult Literacy* and the *ALAN Review*.

This book was composed by Electronic Imaging in Berkeley and Interstate.

Typefaces used on the cover include Trebuchet MS and Zurich Ex BT.

The book was printed on 50-lb. Williamsburg Offset paper by Versa Press, Inc.